New Zealand Novels
and Novelists
1861-1979

New Zealand Novels and Novelists

1861-1979

an annotated bibliography

James Burns

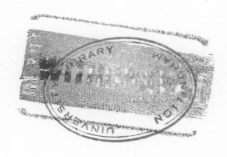

Heinemann

Heinemann Publishers
Cnr College Road and Kilham Avenue, Auckland 9, New Zealand
The Windmill Press, Kingswood, Tadworth, Surrey KT20 6TG, England
4 Front Street, Exeter, New Hampshire 03833, U.S.A.

Also at Edinburgh, Melbourne, Johannesburg, Ibadan,
Nairobi, Lusaka, New Delhi, Hong Kong, Singapore,
Kuala Lumpur, Kingston, Port of Spain

ISBN 0 86863 372 0

© 1981 James Burns
First Published 1981

Printed in Hong Kong

Contents

Acknowledgements

My thanks to the library staffs of Auckland City Council, Auckland Institute & Museum, Manukau City Council, New Zealand National Library Service, Onehunga Borough Council, University of Auckland; and to the following New Zealand authors: M. H. Holcroft, John A. Lee, Dame Ngaio Marsh, Olaf Ruhen and James Sanders.

Introduction

I first became acquainted with New Zealand novels around 1936 and I recall with clarity the two that I then read; they were *Children of the poor* by John A. Lee and *Passport to hell* by Robin Hyde. Both works aroused considerable publicity and discussion. My interest in the New Zealand novel continues undiminished and in the last forty years I have seen its stature so increase that it is now the subject of serious study at our universities.

In quantity too its growth is apparent; in the 1950s, the last decade before television's intrusion into reading time, more than one hundred and thirty novels appeared. In the 1960s the number exceeded three hundred and a similar figure will be attained for the 1970s, bringing to more than a thousand the aggregate of novels in the bibliography.

Judging by their collections, librarians differ about what constitutes a New Zealand novel. My policy here is to include the work of New Zealanders resident abroad, even when a novel is not related to this country, for example *A way of love* by James Courage. Publication in this country does not of itself seem to justify a novel's inclusion; *The tour* by Christopher W. Nixon, published by Reed in Wellington as well as in Sydney and in London, describes a cricket tour by the MCC of Australia and moreover is the work of an Australian author. Nor I feel can Fay Weldon be regarded as a New Zealand writer despite her presence in the New Zealand section of a large public library. On the other hand, it seems unduly restrictive to exclude the work of a person born outside this country who has spent some time here or who is domiciled in New Zealand, when the novel in question is set in this country. It is difficult ultimately to define a boundary. It was not considered justifiable to claim *The Thorn Birds* by Colleen McCullough as a New Zealand novel despite its early chapters; yet the curiosity value of translations of Jules Verne's stories set in and around New Zealand seems to justify their inclusion. Such decisions might give rise to debate, but it seems that an overall criterion must concern the needs and interests of a reading public and researchers alike. Stories written for children were not included.

Library rules governing names of authors, married women and pseudonyms are subject to change and recent usage appears to favour the name by which a person is best known, which is sometimes a matter of opinion. However, there should be no difficulty here in identifying authors or their works.

The annotations with the novels are a brief indication of the content and do not claim to be an assessment. They are not appended to many nineteenth century novels where the alternative or subtitle provides a descriptive guide to the narrative.

Originally my intention with the bibliography was to update my earlier *Twentieth century New Zealand novels 1900-1967*, containing two hundred titles, which was cyclostyled in 1967 for libraries and for students of New Zealand fiction. David Ling of Heinemann Publishers suggested the nineteenth century should not be omitted and strongly recommended that the completed work contain both an author and a title index. As far as I am aware no comprehensive listing of authors has appeared since E. M. Smith's *A history of New Zealand fiction* (Reed, 1939) and this is the first occasion a title index has been published.

The publication dates given in *New Zealand Novels and Novelists 1861-1979* are those of first publication only. For information concerning availability and subsequent republication of New Zealand novels, where this has occurred, it is recommended that the reader consult the latest edition of *New Zealand Books in Print*.

New Zealand Novels 1861-1979

1861

STONEY, Henry Butler. *Taranaki; a tale of the war.* Auckland, Wilson. 128p.

1862

AYLMER, Mrs Isabella. *Distant homes*, or *The Graham family in New Zealand.* London, Griffith & Farran. 183p.

1864

CAMPBELL, Lady. *Martin Tobin.* London, Maxwell. 3 vols.
Early days in the colony.

1865

FARJEON, Benjamin Leopold. *Shadows on the snow; a Christmas story.* Dunedin, Hay. 125p.
Set partly in New Zealand.

1866

FARJEON, Benjamin. *Grif; a story of colonial life.* Dunedin, Hay. vi, 253p.

1867

FAIRBURN, Edwin, pseudonym 'Mohoao'. *The Ships of Tarshish. London, Hall.* 104p.
Planning fast ships.

1868

PYKE, Vincent, wrote as F. E. Renwick. *Lost at the goldfields.* Published in Chamber's Journal. The author was an MP.

VERNE, Jules Gabriel. *Les enfants du capitaine Grant.* Paris. Vol. 3 part 3 is set in New Zealand and there are translations, e.g. *Among the cannibals.* London, Ward, Lock, no date. 192p, illustrations.
After shipwreck survivors are captured by Maoris.

1869

KINGSTON, William Henry Giles. *Holmwood* or *The New Zealand settler.* New York, Griffith & Farran. 69p.

KINGSTON, William. *Waihoura* or *The New Zealand girl.* London, Gall & Inglis. 127p, illustrations.
A Maori girl becomes a Christian.

1872

BARKER, Lady Mary Anne. *A Christmas cake in four quarters.* London, Macmillan. 304p.
Includes New Zealand.

BUTLER, Samuel. *Erewhon* or *Over the range.* London, Trubner. 246p.
This utopia was first published anonymously.

K., J. H. pseudonym. *Henry Ancrum; a tale of the last war in New Zealand.* London, Tinsley. 2 vols.

1873

PYKE, Vincent. *The story of Wild Will Enderby.* Dunedin, Wheeler. vii, 260p.
Life in the goldfields, Dunston area, Otago.

1874

BAINES, William Mortimer ('W.M.B.'). *The narrative of Edward Crewe*, or *Life in New Zealand.* London, S. Low, Marston. 288p.

EVANS, Mrs Charlotte. *Over the hills and far away; a story of New Zealand.* London, S. Low, Marston. 334p.
A 21-year-old joins her father who had preceded her to New Zealand by seven years.

EVANS, Mrs C. *A strange friendship; a story of New Zealand.* London, S. Low, Marston. 247p.
Domestic affairs in the colony.

MARRYATT, Emilia. *Amongst the Maoris; a book of adventure.* London, F. Warne. 366p.

PYKE, Vincent. *The adventures of George Washington Pratt.* Dunedin, Wheeler. iv, 97p.
Goldfields tale.

WHITE, John. *Te Rou* or *The Maori at home.* London, S. Low, Marston. 343p.

WILSON, George Hamish. *Ena* or *The ancient Maori.* London, Smith, Elder. viii, 287p.

1877

WISNIOWSKI, Sygurd. *Tikera* or *Children of the Queen of Oceania.* Translated from the Polish by Jerzy Podstolski; edited and introduced by Dennis McEldowney. Auckland, Auckland University Press and O.U.P. 1972. vi, 311p., map. First edition in book form, Warsaw, Gebethner and Wolff, 1877.
Fiction and autobiography by the author who was in New Zealand 1864-1865 and observed the lives of Maori and pakeha. Historical personages include General Cameron and von Tempsky.

1881

BATHGATE, Alexander. *Waitaruna; a story of New Zealand life.* London, S. Low, Marston. viii, 312p.
Success and failure among the pioneers in Otago.

1882

ELLIS, Ellen E. *Everything is possible to will.* London, published at 63 Fleet Street. viii, 245p.
A moral tale.

1884

PYKE, V., editor. *Craigielinn* by F. E. Renwick, with an introduction by William MacDonald. Dunedin, published for the Ayrshire Association by Joseph Braithwaite. 82p.
Set in Southland. The Association Prize Story.

1885

SHORTLAND, Edward George. *Failed to pass* or *The modern midshipman.* London, Simpkin, Marshall. 151p.
Author a Rear-Admiral.

1886

CHEESMAN, Clara E. *A rolling stone.* London, Bentley. 3 vols.
Domestic romance.

1887

WHITWORTH, Robert P. *Hine-Ra* or *The Maori scout; a romance of the New Zealand war.* Melbourne, W. H. Williams. 132p.

1888

CHAPMAN, R. H., editor. *Mihawhenua; the adventures of a party of tourists amongst a tribe of Maoris discovered in Western Otago.* Dunedin, Wilkie. 197p.

FRASER, A. A. *Raromi* or *The Maori chief's heir.* London, Religious Tract Society. 224p.
Adventures of an ex-seaman.

VERNE, Jules. *Deux ans de vacances.* Paris, Hetzel, 1888. Translations and adaptions, e.g. *Adrift in the Pacific.* London, Sampson Low, Marston. 1951, 142p., illustrations. No date. *A long vacation.* Translated by Olga Marx, illustrated by Victor G. Ambrus. London, Oxford University Press, 1967. 208p.
A number of boys from an Auckland school adrift on a ship reach an uninhabited island.

1889

LANGTON, William. *Mark Anderson; a tale of station life in New Zealand.* Dunedin, Wilkie. 156p.

REED, George McCullagh. *Hunted.* Auckland, Wilson & Horton. 48p.
Irish family and land problems in New Zealand.

ROCK, Gilbert. *By passion driven; a story of a wasted life.* Dunedin, Wilkie. 135p.
Crime in Dunedin.

VOGEL, Sir Julius. *Anno Domini 2000* or *Woman's destiny.* London, Hutchinson. 331p.
Political. Author Prime Minister of N.Z. at 38.

1890

HENTY, George Alfred. *Maori and settler; a story of the New Zealand war.* With eight full-page illustrations by Alfred Pearse and a map. London, Blackie & Son. 352p.

HOOD, Archibald. *Dicky Barrett with his ancient mariners and much more ancient cannon! at the siege of Moturoa: being a realistic story of the rough old times in New Zealand among the turbulent Maoris and the adventurous whalers ere settlement took place...* New Plymouth, at the 'Taranaki Herald' Office. 109p.

WATSON, Henry Brereton Marriott. *The web of the spider.* London, Hutchinson. x, 377p.
Maori wars of the 1860s.

WESTON, Jessie. *Ko Meri* or *A cycle of Cathay.* London, Remington. 394p.
Auckland society and a half-caste girl.

1891

CHAMIER, George T. *Philosopher Dick.* London, Unwin. 2 vols.
A New Zealand shepherd. Sequel, A South Sea siren, *1895.*

COTTLE, Thomas. *Frank Melton's luck* or *Off to New Zealand.* Auckland, H. Brett. 171p.
Farming and goldfields.

FERGUSON, Dugald. *Vicissitudes of bush life in Australia and New Zealand.* London, Sonnenschein. viii, 328p.

MacCARTIE, Justin Charles. *Making his pile; a colonial story.* Melbourne, Mason, Firth & McCutcheon. 295p.
New Zealand and Australia.

1892

CHURCHWARD, William Brown. *Jem Peterkin's daughter; an antipodean novel.* London, Sonnenschein. 3 vols.
Settlers and the Hauhau movement.

HALL, J. ('J.H.L.') *Potona* or *Unknown New Zealand.* Wellington, Wright, Harding. 132p.

WARDON, Reve. *Macpherson's Gully; a tale of New Zealand life.* Christchurch, Simpson & Williams. 55p.
A new immigrant to Lyttleton in the 1870s and unemployed joins the gold rush to the West Coast.

1893

WILSON, Lady Anne Glenny (Adams). *Alice Lauder; a sketch.* London, Osgood, McIlvane. 256p.
Romance about an Australian girl who studies music; partly set in New Zealand.

1894

BAKER, Louisa Alice (Dawson), pseudonym 'Alien'. *A daughter of the King.* London, Hutchinson. viii, 314p.
Women's emancipation.

BULLOCK, Margaret (Carson), pseudonym Tua-O-Rangi. *Utu; a story of love, hate and revenge.* Auckland, Brett. 191p.
A story of Maori and pakeha.

1895

CHAMIER, G. T. *A South Sea siren; a novel descriptive of New Zealand life in the early days.* London, T. F. Unwin. 416p.
A sequel to Philosopher Dick, *1891.*
Well-to-do society and the notorious Mrs Wylde.

TREGEAR, Edward. *Hedged with divinities.* Wellington, Harding. 142p.
'Skit on women's rights' (Hocken).

SCOTT, Robert H. *Ngamihi* or *The rebel chief's daughter; a tale of the war in New Zealand.* Brisbane, Printed by E. A. Howard. 335p., illustrations.

1896

FORDE, H. A. *Across two seas; a New Zealand tale.* London, Wells Gardner, Darton. 188p.
Immigrants arrive in Auckland.

HUME, Fergus. *The expedition of Captain Flick.* London, Jarrold. vi, 363p.
A voyage to the mysterious island of Isk.

NISBET, Hume. *The rebel chief; a romance of New Zealand.* London, F. V. White. xii, 296p.
Conflict between Maoris friendly and those hostile to the settlers.

REED, George McCullagh. *The Angel Isafrel; a story of prohibition in New Zealand.* Auckland, Upton, 100p.

STELIN, Ebba. *A New Zealand pearl.* Wellington, Brown, Thomson. 181p.
Girl on a farm who writes.

WESTBURY, F. Atha. *The shadow of Hilton Fernbrook; a romance of Maoriland.* London, Chatto & Windus. 296p.

1897

ADAMS, R. N. *The counterfeit seal; a tale of Otago's first settlers.* Dunedin, Otago Daily Times. 298p.
Scotland transplanted to Otago.

KACEM, Alie. *For father's sake* or *A tale of New Zealand life.* Wellington, Brown, Thomson. 440p.
The misery caused by liquor.

1898

BAKER, Louisa. *Wheat in the ear.* London, Hutchinson. 376p.
Women's rights.

VOGEL, Harry Benjamin. *A Maori maid.* London, C. A. Pearson. 400p.
Includes goldmining adventures.

1899

BELL, John. *In the shadow of the bush; a New Zealand romance.* London, Sands. 320p.
Life in a bush district of the Wellington province where men and women develop a new township.

BROWNE, Thomas Alexander, pseudonym Rolf Boldrewood. *War to the knife* or *Tangata Maori.* London, Macmillan. 420p.
Maori-Pakeha wars.

1900

KAYE, Mrs Eliza Bannerman. *Haromi; a New Zealand story.* London, J. Clarke. 460p.
Robert Agnew, an artist whose association with a half-caste girl ends in tragedy.

1901

BROWN, John Macmillan, pseudonym Geoffrey Sweven. *Riallaro; the archipelago of the exiles.* London, Putnam. 420p.
Visit to a mystic region south-east of Oceania.

BUTLER, Samuel. *Erewhon revisited; twenty years later by both the original discoverer and his son.* London, Grant Richards. xi, 337p.

TAYLOR, Ellen. *A thousand pities.* London, T. Fisher Unwin. 183p.
A romance on a North Island sheep station.

1902

SATCHELL, William. *The land of the lost; a tale of the New Zealand gum country.* London, Methuen. 310p.
Diverse characters around Hokianga in the 1890s.

WALKER, William Sylvester. *Zealandia's guerdon.* London, John Long. 328p.
The story by an Australian-born author covers many facets of New Zealand life.

1903

BROWN, John Macmillan. *Limanora; the island of progress.* London, Putnam. ix, 711p.
Utopia, strongly scientific.

HODDER, William Reginald. *The daughter of the dawn; a realistic story of Maori magic.* London, Jarrold. 333p.

MAKGILL, Sir George, editor. *Outside and overseas. . .* London, Methuen. xi, 308p, map.
Captain Mungo Ballas in the Auckland area in the early days.

1904

ADAMS, Arthur Henry. *Tussock land: a romance of New Zealand and the Commonwealth.* London, F. Unwin. 311p.
A pakeha's love for a part-Maori girl.

BELL, George William. *Mr Oseba's last discovery.* Wellington, N.Z. Times Co. 255p, illustrations.
The author, a U.S. Consul in Sydney, visited N.Z. in 1903 and describes the most sturdy democracy civilisation had ever produced.

1905

INGLEWOOD, Kathleen, Kate Evelyn (Isitt). *Patmos.* London, Gordon & Gotch. 352p.
The struggle for prohibition of liquor.

McADAM, Constance (Clyde), wrote as Constance Clyde. *A pagan's love.* London, T. Fisher Unwin. 312p.
Freedom for women.

OWEN, Charles. *Captain Sheen; a romance of New Zealand history.* London, T. Fisher Unwin. 311p.
A young man sails to New Zealand with a rogue captain and they clash with Te Rauparaha.

SATCHELL, W. *The toll of the bush.* London, Methuen. 422p.
Pioneer life in Northland. 'His best novel' (McCormick).

1907

HORSELY, Reginald Ernest. *In the grip of the hawk; a story of the Maori wars.* London, T. C. & E. C. Jack. xi, 243p.
Te Kooti, the Hauhaus and the struggle between Maori and Pakeha.

LYTTLETON, Edith Joan, pseudonym G. B. Lancaster. *The tracks we tread.* New York, Doubleday, Page. 302p.
The lives of station hands on big sheep runs.

SATCHELL, W. *The elixir of life.* London, Chapman & Hall. 320p.
A shipwreck on an uninhabited island and a cure-all serum.

1908

GRACE, Alfred Augustus. *Atareta, the belle of the Kainga.* Wellington, Gordon & Gotch. 93p.
Mission educated Maori girl has problems getting married.

KOEBEL, William Henry. *The anchorage; the story of a New Zealand sheep farm.* London, F. Griffiths. 311p.
Ronald Calverton is a new immigrant and a loner.

LYTTLETON, Edith. *The altar stairs.* London, Hodder & Stoughton. viii, 324p.
The altar stairs lead to God; a missionary and a trader in Melanesia.

MACTIER, Susie (Susan Seaman). *The hills of Hauraki* or *The unequal yoke; a story of New Zealand life.* London, Sunday School Union. 230p.
Marriage and liquor.

1909

DEVERELL, Evangeline. *Eve Stanley of New Zealand.* London, Ouseley. 224p.
Romance in Auckland.

VOGEL, Harry. *The tragedy of a flirtation.* London, Greening. 312p.
A girl comes from England to marry a man and discovers he has a Maori mistress.

1910

GROSSMANN, Edith Howitt (Searle). *The heart of the bush.* London, Sands. 334p.
Marriage dilemma for an educated woman.

1911

MACTIER, S. *Miranda Stanhope.* Auckland, Brett Printing Co. 188p, portrait.
Three adult sisters migrate to New Zealand.

PLATTS, Herbert Walton. *The shifter.* London, Whitcombe & Tombs. 285p.
A sea romance, with mutiny.

REEVES, Amber (pseudonym of Mrs White). *The reward of virtue.* London, Heinemann. 309p.
Romance in England.

1912

ADAMS, A. H. *A touch of phantasy; a romance for those who are lucky enough to wear glasses.* London, John Lane. 304p.
A man who worked in an office in Sydney and the girls he knew.

FERGUSON, Dugald. *Mates.* London, Hodder & Stoughton. 509p.
Australian backblocks and Otago goldfields.

1913

FERGUSON, Carlyle. *Marie Levant.* Wellington, Whitcombe & Tombs. 205p.
A ship going to Campbell Island in the 1830s.

REES, Arthur John. *The merry marauders.* London, Heinemann, 258p.
New Zealand theatre tour.

1914

GRACE, A. A. *The tale of a timber town.* Sydney, Gordon & Gotch. 184p.
Maungatapu murders of the 1860s, a trial and the goldfields. First published in 'The Otago Witness'.

SATCHELL, W. *The greenstone door.* London, Sidgwick & Jackson. 398p.
Background is the Maori-Pakeha war.

1915

HELLIER, F. *Colonials in khaki.* London, Murray & Eveden. 127p.
'Three New Zealanders, two girls and a man cross the Pacific and America to England where the man enlists for World War 1 and the girls return, bringing the wounded brother of one of them.' Times Literary Supplement *10 August 1916.*

1916

BEDFORD, H. Louisa. *Under one standard* or *The touch that makes us kin; a story of the time of the Maori war.* Illustrated by Harold Piffard. London, Society for the Promotion of Christian Knowledge. 223p.

CHURCH, Hubert Newman Wigmore. *Tonks.* London, Holden & Hardingham. 304p.
A man makes a tour of New Zealand concealing his true identity.

THORNTON, Guy. *The wowser; a tale of the New Zealand bush.* London, Kingsgate Press. 351p.

1917

HALES, Alfred Greenwood. *McGlusky's great adventure.* London, Hodder and Stoughton, 1917, 283p, illustrated.
An elderly Scot working for some years in New Zealand is deemed unsuitable for the army, later becomes a seaman and participates in the Gallipoli campaign.

MUSGROVE, H. *Myola.* London, Hodder &
Stoughton. 308p.
*Myola is the daughter of an English nobleman with a
bad reputation in the colony. Second prize in Hodder's
competition.*

1918

FUSSELL, James Coldham. *Corporal Tikitanu, V.C.*
Auckland, Worthington. 52p, illustrations.
World War I.

GIBBONS, Margaret (Macgill). *An Anzac's bride.*
London, H. Jenkins. 320p.
Romance of NZ soldier and English girl.

PEACOCKE, Isabel Maud (Mrs Cluett). *Cinderella's
suitors.* London, Ward, Lock. 318p.
Romance of an Auckland typist.

1919

OWEN, Jean Allan (Pinder). *Under palm and pine.*
London, Society for the Promotion of Christian
Knowledge. 128p.
A man escapes from a French ship to New Zealand.

1920

HUNTER, Edward. *The road the men came home.*
London, National Labour Press. 140p.
*A young coal miner from Scotland comes to New
Zealand and is a force in trade union affairs.*

MANDER, (Mary) Jane. *The story of a New Zealand
river.* New York, Lane. 423p.
*Emancipation of a woman living in a Northland
timber-milling area.*

PEACOCKE, Isabel. *The guardian.* London, Ward,
Locke. 319p.
*A rural romance about the people who live at a home-
stead called Wharemoana.*

1921

FOSTON, Herman. *At the front; a story of pluck
and heroism in the railway construction camps in the
Dominion of New Zealand.* London, Arthur H.
Stockwell. vii, 231p, illustrations.
Christianity battling against the evils of liquor.

McKENZIE, Sir Clutha Nantes. *The tale of a
trooper.* London, Lane. 200p.
Includes the Gallipoli campaign.

MANDER, Jane. *The passionate puritan.* New York,
Lane. 308p.
*A young woman teacher in a Maori-Pakeha area of
Northland.*

1922

MANDER, Jane. *The strange attraction.* New York,
Dodd, Mead. 376p.
*An independent young woman in journalism in
Northland.*

OSMOND, Sophie. *Ponga Bay; a story of old New
Zealand.* London, Hutchinson. 286p.
Romance of Maori war period.

1923

PEACOCKE, Isabel. *The adopted family.* London,
Ward, Lock. 320p, illustrations.
*Mainly the adventures of some children staying in the
country.*

SAFRONI-MIDDLETON, Arnold. *Ragged romance;
out of the sapphire seas and tropic lands.* London,
Jarrolds. 252p.
*A late 19th century sentimental wanderer in New
Zealand, Samoa, Papua and the Marquesas.*

1924

CARMAN, Dulce. *The broad stairway.* London,
J. M. Ousely & Son. 285p.
*A woman recalls a message she heard as a child and
discovers a fortune.*

EMERY, J. Inman. *The tiger of Baraguna.* London,
Jarrolds. 322p.
*A mystery story includes the Maharaja of Baraguna.
The author was a resident of Auckland.*

GIBSON, Harry Thomas. *That Gibbie galoot; the tale
of a teacher* by H.T.G. Auckland, NZ Observer
Printing Works. 166p.
Humorous experiences not confined to teaching.

REES, Rosemary Frances. *April's sowing.* London,
Herbert Jenkins. 312p.
*A girl from England goes to New Zealand and is
associated with an alcoholic.*

REES, Rosemary. *Heather of the south.* London,
Jenkins. 311p.
Romance on a dairy farm.

1925

COOK, Harvey Harold. *Far flung; a New Zealand
story.* London, Long. 318p.
Life in the backblocks.

MANDER, Jane. *Allen Adair.* London, Hutchinson.
288p.
*An unhappy marriage in Northland gum country in
the late 19th century.*

REES, Rosemary. *The lake of enchantment.* London, Herbert Jenkins. 312p.
Romance for a writer and actress living quietly in the South Island.

1926

ALLEN, Charles Richard. *Brown smock; the tale of a tune.* London, Warne. 275p.
Development of a musician in England.

DEVANNY, Jean (Jane?) (Crooks). *The butcher shop.* London, Duckworth. 313p.
A woman's frank attitude to sex, and some grim incidents. The novel was banned in New Zealand.

DEVANNY, Jean. *Lenore Divine.* London, Duckworth. 320p.
A young woman in Wellington who works as a journalist and promotes socialism falls in love with a Maori.

KERR, Walter. *Our home in the roaring forties.* Napier, Ball. 141p.
Early days in the colony.

MANDER, Jane. *The besieging city; a novel of New York.* London, Hutchinson. 280p.
Intellectuals at work and play and in sex roles.

1927

ALLEN, C. *Tarry knight! a study in stained glass.* London, J. Hamilton. 256p.
A dean and his family in England.

BOLITHO, Henry Hector. *Solemn boy.* London, Chatto & Windus. 316p.
Timothy Shrove, growing up in New Zealand and Australia, becomes a journalist.

COOK, H. *The cave of Endor; a New Zealand story.* London, Long. 318p.
The cave is that of a tohunga.

REES, Rosemary. *Life's what you make it.* London, Wright & Brown. 256p.
A romance in a fishing area in Rotorua.

1928

DEVANNY, Jean. *Dawn beloved.* London, Duckworth. 352p.
The life of Dawn: girlhood, marriage and tragedy.

HOLCROFT, Montague Harry. *Beyond the Breakers.* London, Long. 288p.
A conflict on a South Pacific island plantation owned by a German with three sons; a beautiful nurse and a castaway.

MANDER, Jane. *Pins and pinnacles.* London, Hutchinson. 288p.
Mirabel Heath, a writer in South Kensington, London.

SMYTH, Walter. *Jean of the tussock country.* London, Mills & Boon. 246p.
A New Zealand romance with a backblocks setting.

1929

BOLITHO, H. *Judith Silver.* London, Knopf. 248p.
A New Zealander at Cambridge University, his father mentally ill, and Judith Silver an opera singer.

BROWNE, Charles Robert Barton. *Maori witchery; native life in New Zealand.* London, Dent. 209p.
'The two races can never assimilate' (Author).

DEVANNY, Jean. *Riven.* London, Duckworth. 320p.
A family with a woman who has a passion to mother everybody.

GORDON, Mona Clifton. *Torn tapestry.* London, Wright. 388p.
The story of the Thornleigh family, 1798-1928, mainly in New Zealand.

HOLCROFT, M. *The flameless fire.* London, John Long. 288p.
An industrial chemist in Java and Australia has an opium problem.

SMYTH, Walter. *Bonzer Jones.* London, Mills & Boon. 254p.
A girl who inherits 50 000 acres is being bluffed into selling the property when Bonzer Jones comes to the rescue.

1930

ACHESON, Frank Oswald Victor. *Plume of the Arawas.* Christchurch, Whitcombe & Tombs. 308p, illustrations.
Maori life and conflicts in pre-European times.

BOLITHO, H. *The flame on Ethirdova.* London, Cobden-Sanderson. 218p.
Life in a European valley and its monastery.

BOSWORTH, Isabel. *A trip to New Zealand.* London, London Publishing Company. viii, 216p, port., illustrations.
Only half of this 'travelogue' set in New Zealand.

DEVANNY, Jean. *Bushman Burke.* London, Duckworth. 320p. Abridged version *Wages of desire* published in Sydney by Frank Johnson; also published as *Taipo?*
A former boxer inherits money that changes his life.

DEVANNY, Jean. *Devil made saint.* London, Duckworth. 320p.
A study of a composer and his marriage.

LLOYD, Victor Stanton. *Son of Peter*. E. Nash & Grayson. 288p.
Personal and business life of the owner of a chain of footwear stores in London.

SMYTH, Walter. *Wooden rails; a romance of the timberlands*. London, Mills & Boon. 254p.
The love interests of a girl from the bush, her dreams and disappointments.

1931

GREENWOOD, Helene (Fodor). *The splendid horizon; a novel of New Zealand life*. London, Cranton. 284p.
Partly spiritualism.

HOLCROFT, M. *Brazilian daughter*. London, Long. 287p.
A man and his twenty-five year old daughter he hasn't seen. Set in England and Brazil.

HOLDER, William Graeme. *The decker*. London, Lane. 310p.
Mystery and romance in Auckland.

REES, Rosemary. *Sane Jane*. London, Chapman & Hall. 338p. Published in 1940 in New York, Arcadia House, under the title *Second romance*.
A New Zealand girl in London interested in the theatre.

SCANLAN, Nelle Margaret. *Primrose Hill*. London, Jarrold. 288p.
People living in London.

SCANLAN, Nelle. *The top step*. London, Jarrold. 288p.
An elderly bachelor in England marries a widow with two children.

1932

DEVANNY, Jean. *Poor swine*. London, Duckworth. 285p.
The life of a woman married to a miner at Denniston.

FERGUSON, Henry. *Harpoon*. London, Newnes. 244p.
Whaling in Antarctic waters in the 1920s.

LUSK, Elizabeth (Rees), pseudonym Elizabeth Milton. *They called her Faith*. London, Wright & Brown. 252p.
The Bay of Islands in the 1840s is the setting for a romance with a missionary's daughter.

RAY, James. *The scene is changed*. London, John Heritage. 294p.
A New Zealand Rhodes Scholar in England.

SCANLAN, Nelle. *Pencarrow*. London, Jarrold. 320p.
The first of four novels on the Pencarrow family, covering the nineteenth and twentieth centuries. The author was the first local novelist to be widely read in New Zealand.

1933

BAUME, Frederic Ehrenfried, wrote as Eric Baume. *Half-caste*. Sydney, Macquarie. 251p. Revised edition, London, Falcon Press, 1950. 212p.
A part-Maori girl from a rural area, at 14 goes to a white boarding school in Auckland and later marries an Englishman.

COURAGE, James Francis. *One house*. London, Gollancz. 207p.
The lives of four unmarried sisters living in England, are changed by a 'gentleman caller'.

DRESCHFELT, Mrs, wrote as Prudence Cadey. *Broken pattern*. With a foreword by Stephen Gwynn. London, Fenland Press. 359p.
After marriage in England a couple emigrate to New Zealand and find the conditions discouraging. The man has a drink problem.

HOLDER, W. G. *Restless earth*. Auckland, Associated NZ Authors' Publishing Company. 255p. First published in the 'Stratford Evening Post' under the title *When the earth shook* in 1931.
Romance set in New Plymouth also covers the Napier earthquake of 1931.

LYTTLETON, Edith. *Pageant*. Sydney, Endeavour Press; London, Allen & Unwin. 416p.
A family chronicle set in nineteenth century Tasmania; it created great interest in Australia.

SCANLAN, Nelle. *Tides of youth*. London, Jarrold. 288p.
Continues the Pencarrow story.

TATE, Robert Desmond. *The doughman*. Sydney, Endeavour Press. 228p.
Death at the bakehouse.

1934

BAUME, Eric. *Burnt sugar*. Sydney, Macquarie Head Press. 398p.
Race problems for Italians in Queensland.

BERROW, Norman. *The smokers of hashish*. London, Eldon Press. 285p.
Romance and mystery in Morocco.

HOGG, James Wilson. *Snow man*. London, John Long, 288p.
The harm caused by the drug traffic.

JEPSON, Margaret. *Via Panama.* London, Hamish Hamilton. 283p.
People on a ship from Southampton to Wellington.

KENNY, Alice Annie. *The rebel.* Sydney, Macquarie. 300p.
Seventeen-year-old Prudence rebels against a strict Victorian father.

LEE, John Alexander. *Children of the poor.* London, Laurie. 255p. Sequel *The hunted*, 1936.
First-person narrative of the childhood of Albany Porcello in Otago. The work was first published anonymously and created much disturbance.

LUSK, Elizabeth. *Strange horizon.* London, Wright & Brown. 252p.
Following marriage a couple leave for England where the wife has difficulties with her husband's relations.

MARSH, Dame (Edith) Ngaio. *A man lay dead.* London, Bles. 287p.
A house party in England and the Murder Game provides work for Detective-Inspector Alleyn in the author's first crime novel. The reviewer in the Times Literary Supplement *17 May 1934 presumed the writer was a man.*

MULGAN, Alan Edward. *Spur of morning.* London, Dent. vii, 364p.
Career of a journalist-politician at the turn of the century.

SCANLAN, Nelle. *Winds of heaven.* London, Jarrold. 328p.
More of the Pencarrow family.

SCOTT, Mary Edith (Clarke). *Where the apple reddens* by Marten Stuart (pseudonym). London, Hurst & Blackett. 288p.
A prosperous farmer, a widower, is the father of his Maori housekeeper's child.

1935

ADAIR, Hazel. Pseudonym of Hazel Iris Addis (Wilson). *Wanted, a son.* London, Hutchinson. 287p.
A romance set in England and New Zealand involving four sisters.

DEVANNY, Jean. *The virtuous courtesan.* New York, Macaulay. 285p.
The marriage of a dancer in Sydney.

GUTHRIE, John. Pseudonym of John Brodie. *The little country.* London, Nelson. xii, 413p.
Satire on aspects of New Zealand life.

HANSEN, Ole Conrad. *Reisen til New Zealand.* Oslo, Tiden norsh forlag. 112p. Forord (preface) signed Aksel Sandemose. Apparently no English trans-lation but the Auckland Institute and Museum Library has a German translation. Ole Hansen's *Reise nach Neu-Seeland*, von ihm selbst erzählt; bebildert von Olaf Gulbransson. München, C. H. Beck, 1936. 104p. On the verso: Aus dem norwegischen übertragen von A. W. Schilling. (Hansen's *Journey to New Zealand*, narrated by himself; illustrated by Gulbransson, translated from the Norwegian by Schilling.)
A Norwegian in New Zealand at the end of the last century.

MARSH, Ngaio. *Enter a murderer.* London, Geoffrey Bles. 284p.
A crime is committed on the stage of the Unicorn Theatre but fortunately Inspector Alleyn is in the audience.

MARSH, Ngaio and Dr Henry Jellett. *The nursing home murder.* London, Bles. 286p.
Why did the future Dame require the assistance of a medical man? In later reprints of the work Jellett's name is omitted.

SCANLAN, Nelle. *Ambition's harvest.* London, Jarrold. 288p.
A girl inherits some money from her aunt and travels to the United States.

SCOTT, Mary. *And shadows flee* by Marten Stuart (pseudonym). London, Hurst and Blackett. 288p.
Margaret O'Neill, a convict, escapes from Australia to New Zealand.

WHYTE, Anna D. *Change your sky; a novel.* London, Hogarth Press. 302p.
English people in Florence.

1936

ALLEN, C. R. *A poor scholar; a tale of progress.* Wellington, Reed. 287p.
From poor circumstances in Dunedin, a boy sub-sequently becomes a Rhodes Scholar.

ANTHONY, Frank Sheldon. *Follow the call.* (A posthumous novel with a memoir of the author.) Wellington, Reed, 187p. First appeared in the 'Christchurch Weekly Press', 1924.
Experiences of former soldier turned farmer, told with some humour.

CLAPPERTON, Annie Ada (Reeves). *The Lauder Brothers, New Zealand.* Wellington, Reed. 252p.
Pioneering experiences.

DEVANNY, Jean. *Sugar heaven.* Sydney, Modern Publishers. 317p.
Sugar workers and Weil's disease in Queensland.

ESCOTT, Margaret. *Show down.* London, Chatto & Windus. 270p. Also New York, Norton, under the title *I told my love.*
A New Zealand farmer and an English woman marry but wish to live free.

GUTHRIE, John. *So they began.* London, Nelson. viii, 374p.
Pioneering days in Taranaki from the 1830s.

HODGE, Merton (Horace Emerton Hodge). *The wind and the rain.* London, Cassell. 327p.
Based on his successful play of the same title about student life in Edinburgh. The author was a doctor and he acknowledges the help of Pamela Frankau in the novelisation of the play.

HOLCROFT, Montague. *The Papuan; a novel of a strange dramatic adventure.* (*In* 'The Bulletin', Sydney, 20 May 1936-22 July 1936.)
A woman doctor in Papua and England and the men in love with her.

HYDE, Robin. Pseudonym of Iris Guiver Wilkinson.
Check to your King; the life history of Charles, Baron de Thierry, King of Nukahiva, Sovereign Chief of New Zealand. London, Hurst & Blackett. 288p.
Acclaimed historical novel on the Baron who died in Auckland in 1864 aged about 71.

HYDE, Robin. *Passport to hell.* London, Hurst & Blackett. 256p.
The story of John Douglas Stark, 'Starkie', a tough soldier in World War I. Sequel Nor the years condemn, *1938.*

LEE, John. *The hunted.* London, Laurie. 257p.
Sequel to *Children of the poor.*
Teenager Porcello at a boys' reformatory at Burnham around 1900.

MACDONALD, Sheila (Mackenzie), later Mrs S. S. Moore. *The tune and the dancer.* London, Cassell. 319p.
A young English woman teacher goes to South Africa and Southern Rhodesia. The author, who went to Rhodesia before World War I, was the daughter of South Island MP Scobie Mackenzie.

MARSH, Ngaio. *Death in ecstasy.* London, Bles. 320p, plan.
In a London church a woman drinks wine and dies.

REES, Rosemary. *Miss Tiverton's shipwreck; a novel.* London, Chapman & Hall. 250p.
Passengers from a steam ship spend some time on an uninhabited island in the Pacific.

SCANLAN, Nelle. *The marriage of Nicholas Cotter.* London, Hale. 284p.
An unmarried English lawyer approaching fifty falls in love with an 18-year-old girl.

SMITH, Harry Gilmore. *New Zealand calling.* New Plymouth, Avery. 366p.
The people between the World Wars as seen by an English major and his ex-airman nephew.

WEST, Joyce. *The sheep kings.* Wellington, H. H. Tombs. 258p.
Story of the King family from the 1830s includes marriage to a part-Maori girl.

WHYTE, Anna D. *Lights are bright.* London, Hogarth Press. 320p.
A shipboard romance for a man coming to New Zealand. In Wellington he encounters a journalist and an earthquake.

WRIGHT, Stanley Sherman. *Oak uprooted; a romance of early New Zealand.* London, Skeffington. 288p.
Involves a former convict from Australia.

1937

ALLEN, C. R. *The hedge-sparrow.* Wellington, Reed. 255p.
From an unpromising background a man qualifies in law and enters politics.

HEWETT, Joan Evelyne. *A divorce has been arranged.* London, Duckworth. 295p.
Matrimonial discord.

HYDE, Robin. *Wednesday's children.* London, Hurst & Blackett. 286p.
Fantasy and humour predominate in this tale of Wednesday who wins a fortune in a lottery and purchases an island.

LEE, John. *Civilian into soldier.* London, Laurie. 295p.
John Guy is a volunteer who saw action on the Western Front in World War I.

MARSH, Ngaio. *Vintage murder.* London, Bles. 275p, diagram.
Detective Alleyn in New Zealand investigating a murder in a theatre.

SCANLAN, Nelle. *Leisure for living.* London, Hale. 416p.
Tells of the Copeland family of Palmerston North. The two brothers consider working hard all day a waste of life.

1938

ANTHONY, Frank. *Me and Gus.* Hawera, Hawera Star Publishing Company. 100p.
Two mates on run-down farms in Taranaki in comic situations.

HYDE, Robin. *The godwits fly.* London, Hurst & Blackett. 296p.
Hannay family in Wellington; Eliza a portrait of the author.

HYDE, Robin. *Nor the years condemn.* London, Hurst & Blackett. 352p. Sequel to *Passport to hell.*
Stark is now a civilian.

LAWLOR, Patrick Anthony. *The house of Templemore.* Wellington, Reed. 257p. A new chapter 'Daniel Mahoney's secret' of 28 pages published separately in 'NZ Tablet'.
Family, schooling and young manhood of Terry Mahoney.

LYTTLETON, Edith Joan. *Promenade.* Sydney, Angus & Robertson. 275p.
An Auckland family in the second half of the nineteenth century; social life and Maori wars.

MARSH, Ngaio. *Artists in crime.* London, Bles. 310p.
Agatha Troy, Alleyn's wife, discusses with students in her art studio how a model could be killed.

MARSH, Ngaio. *Death in a white tie.* London, Bles. 319p, diagram.
The mysterious death of Lord Gospell in a taxi.

RAWLINSON, Gloria. *Music in the listening place.* London, Cassell. ix, 277p.
Maoris and Europeans appear in this part-fantasy tale.

REES, Rosemary. *Sing a song of Sydney; a novel.* London, Chapman & Hall. 319p.
People in the theatre in Australia.

SCANLAN, Nelle. *A guest of life.* London, Hale. 416p.
After leaving school two young Pommies try their luck in the land of opportunity — New Zealand.

1939

ALLEN, C. R. *The young pretender.* London, Massie. 391p.
When a singer dies, his son is cared for by three bachelors.

ELLIOTT, Sir James Sands. *The hundred years.* London, Hale. 320p.
Historical, covering New Zealand from the 1830s.

HAYWARD, Rudall Charles Victor and Alexander Wyclif Reed. *Rewi's last stand* by A. W. Reed. Based on the film scenario by Rudall C. Hayward. Wellington, Reed. 175p, illustrations.
Trouble between Maoris and pakehas in the Waikato.

McCARTHY, Beryl. *Castles in the soil.* Wellington, Reed. 335p.
Two brothers and descendants covering 19th and 20th centuries. Includes interracial love.

MARSH, Ngaio. *Overture to death.* London, Bles. 316p.
A life is extinguished unexpectedly in a village hall where a play is being staged.

MULGAN, John Alan Edward. *Man alone.* London, Selwyn and Blount. 206p.
Study of isolated man between the wars as represented by an English immigrant to New Zealand.

SCANLAN, Nelle. *Kelly Pencarrow.* London, Hale. 352p.
Sequel to Winds of heaven, *this fourth and final novel of the Pencarrow series takes the story almost up to World War II.*

1940

EDEN, Dorothy. *Singing shadows.* London, Paul. 287p.
History and romance in the young colony.

MARSH, Ngaio. *Death at the bar.* London, Collins for the Crime Club. 284p.
Drinks and darts at a pub subsequently lead to a coroner's inquest.

MARSH, Ngaio. *Death of a peer.* Boston, Little, Brown. viii, 374p, diagram. Published in London by Collins, 1941, under the title *Surfeit of Lampreys.*
The death of a nobleman in London leads to investigations by Fox and Alleyn.

REES, Rosemary. *Hetty looks for local colour.* London, Wright & Brown. 288p.
A woman of thirty, after winning some money, gives up her London job for a quiet place to write.

RICHMOND, Mary. *Poison weed.* London, Wright & Brown. 284p.
The other woman poisons the wife.

SADD, Norman (pseudonym). *The transgressions of Aolele.* Auckland, Pearson. 314p.
Covers 19th century (Maori Wars) and the 20th century when Aolele, a convent-trained girl, is in love with a half-caste who is charged with manslaughter.

WHITE, John. *Revenge; a love tale of the Mount Eden tribe.* Edited by A. W. Reed. Wellington, Reed. xviii, 289p, port.
The Maori in pre-European times.

1941

FLAXMAN, Anna. *Hinemoa*. London, Peter Davies. 279p.
A young girl growing up in New Zealand and elsewhere.

MYERS, Martha Washington. *Valiant love*. Wellington, Reed. 223p.
A Maori school teacher marries a white farmer whose interest in Maori land tenure leads him to study law.

QUENTIN, Dorothy Batten (pseudonym Linda Beverly). *Errand of mercy*. London, Locke. 288p.
A romance.

STAPLES, *Marjory Charlotte (Jefcoate). (Wrote as Rosaline Redwood.) Mocking shadows; a novel.* London, Arthur H. Stockwell. 258p.
An unmarried immigrant couple on a farm in the South Island following a shipwreck in the last century.

WILLIAMS, Harley (John Hargreaves Harley). *Fingal's box*. London, Cape. 382p.
A romance involving a New Zealand medical student.

1942

DEVANNY, Jean. *The killing of Jacqueline Love*. Sydney, F. Johnson. 157p.
Love and violence in the Australian outback.

MARSH, *Ngaio. Death and the dancing footman.* London, Collins for the Crime Club. 320p.
Jonathan Royal, an elderly bachelor, invites guests to his large estate for the weekend.

WHITE, Nelia (Gardner). *Daughter of time; the life of Katherine Mansfield in novel form*. London, Constable. 244p, portrait.

1943

BURDON, Randall Mathews. *Outlaw's progress; a novel of New Zealand*. Wellington, Progressive Publishing Company. 72p.
Based on the Graham manhunt, 1941. See also Erik de Mauny (1949) The huntsman in his career.

FULLARTON, John Haydn. *Troop target*. London, Hutchinson, 1943 or 1944. 224p.
New Zealanders in the Middle East during World War II.

LEE, John A. *The Yanks are coming*. London, Laurie. 192p.
Thriller about two New Zealanders at the time of Pearl Harbour smuggled out of Auckland and later rescued by the US Navy.

LYNN, David (pseudonym of D. McLennan). *The Cobblestone family*. London, Kangaroo Books. 223p.
Social activities around a farming area in Canterbury.

MARSH, Ngaio. *Colour scheme*. London, Collins for the Crime Club. 256p.
Death by unnatural causes at a hot springs resort in the North Island.

SARGESON, Frank. *That summer*. In *Penguin new writing* numbers 17, 18, 19; also in *That summer and other stories*, London, Lehmann, 1946.
After tossing in a farm job a man with itchy feet has a spell in town and is picked up by the police.

1944

GOUDGE, Elizabeth. *Green dolphin country*. London, Hodder & Stoughton. vii, 503p.
Mainly 19th century New Zealand by a writer who had not visited the country but acknowledged a debt to F. E. Maning's Old New Zealand *published in 1863. Filmed in England 1947.*

GRIEVE, Mrs Hamilton. *Spring manoeuvres*. London, Hale. 236p.
A landscape painter unexpectedly acquires a castle near Wellington that arouses national concern.

LEE, J. A. *Shining with the Shiner*. Hamilton, F. W. Mead, i.e. Bonds. 145p.
A tramp who lived on his wits around New Zealand.

MARSH, Ngaio. *Died in the wool*. London, Collins, Crime Club. 254p.
A body is discovered in a bale of wool.

SCANLAN, Nelle. *March moon*. London, Hale. 307p.
A family story set in rural Marlborough.

WILSON, Helen Mary (Ostler). *Moonshine; a story of the eighties*. Wellington, Reed. 160p.
Rural life.

1945

DAVIN, Daniel Marcus. *Cliffs of fall*. London, Nicholson & Watson. 188p.
A young man rebels against a restrictive background to the extent of committing murder.

LAWSON, Will. *The lady of the heather*. Sydney, Angus & Robertson. ix, 160p.
A grand-daughter of Bonnie Prince Charlie, exiled in the 1820s to Campbell Island.

SARGENT, Winston. *The palms bend down*. Christchurch, Caxton Press. 254p.
Based on the diaries of a New Zealand soldier in World War II.

SARGESON, Frank. *When the wind blows.* Christ-church, Caxton Press. 91p. First published in *Penguin new writing*, numbers 27 and 28; is also the first part of *I saw in my dream*, 1949.
Restrictive puritan upbringing of Henry Griffiths and later his employment with a lawyer.

UREN, Martyn. *They will arise; an epic of Greece under the Axis.* Auckland, Collins. 218p.
A New Zealand soldier after the evacuation, with the civilian population and the resistance.

1946

BOLITHO, Hector. *No humour in my love, and two other stories.* London, Herbert Jenkins. 221p.
The rewriting of three novels. No humour in my love (Solemn boy) *pp9-93;* Judith Silver, *pp94-166;* The flame of Ethirdova, *pp167-221.*

LAWSON, Will. *Forbidden gold.* Auckland, Oswald-Sealy. 181p.
The discovery of gold in an ancient Maori burial ground at Terawhiti near Wellington brings misfortune.

MOUNTAIN, Julian. *The pioneers; a romance.* Malvern, Tantivity Press. 181p.
A family over three generations in the second half of the 19th century.

PEACOCK, Isabel. *London called them.* London, Ward, Locke. 223p.
A New Zealand girl goes to London to make good as a writer.

SCANLAN, Nelle. *Kit Carmichael.* London, Hale. 292p.
Chatty novel set in London where Kit gets married.

WEST-WATSON, Keith. *Achmet and the colonel.* London, Lutterworth. 155p.
A story of World War II, with a young Egyptian aiding British Intelligence.

1947

BAUME, Eric. *Mercia Wade.* London, Hutchinson. 187p.
On a ship in mid-Atlantic a woman informs her husband she wants a divorce to marry an American doctor.

DAVIN, Dan. *For the rest of our lives.* London, Nicholson & Watson. 397p.
New Zealand soldiers in North Africa in World War II.

GRIEVE, Hamilton. *Something in the country air.* London, Museum Press. 224p.
Romance was in the air when an ex-serviceman became a rouseabout on a farm.

MARSH, Ngaio. *Final curtain.* London, Collins for the Crime Club. 257p.
Alleyn's wife Agatha Troy does a portrait of a famous actor knight, Sir Henry Ancred.

REES, Rosemary. *Penelope waits, a novel.* London, Chapman & Hall. 246p.
A young Englishman goes to New Zealand to make good.

WALSH, Mrs Hazel. *The fourth point of the star.* Auckland, Printed at the Griffin Press. 136p.
A nurse must never reveal a secret entrusted by a patient, but what about murder?

1948

BALLANTYNE, David Watt. *The Cunninghams.* New York, Vanguard Press. ix, 295p.
Family tensions among mother, father, son, in a study of a small New Zealand town.

BAUME, Eric. *Devil Lord's daughter.* Sydney, Invincible Press. 244p.
Partly based on Captain Cook, and a woman masquerading as a man.

CARMAN, Dulce. *Neath the Maori moon; a New Zealand romance.* London, Wright & Brown. 253p.
A girl with a Maori mother comes to New Zealand from England to assimilate Maori culture.

COURAGE, James. *The fifth child.* London, Constable. 216p.
Matrimonial troubles of well-to-do Mrs Warner expecting a fifth child. She is in the city while her husband manages the sheep farm.

EDEN, Dorothy. *The schoolmaster's daughters.* London, Macdonald. 239p.
A country schoolmaster in England, and a novelist.

FINLAYSON, Roderick David. *Tidal creek.* Sydney, Angus & Robertson. 224p.
Uncle Ted and nephew in a quiet rural community.

MACKENZIE, Andrew Carr. *The house at the estuary.* London, Ward, Lock. 224p.
Murder in London high society.

MERGENDAHL, Charles Henry. *This spring of love.* New York, Doubleday. 253p.
United States troops in New Zealand and the Pacific in World War II.

MOUNTAIN, Julian. *Love is vanity; a novel.* Malvern, England, The Tantivity Press. 226p. *After university a young man with ideals and ideas enters journalism and later becomes interested in religion; the setting is Godsholme (Christchurch?), the most English city in the Dominion of New Zealand.*

O'SULLIVAN, Katherine (Morgan). *The loves of Dretta Gray* by Kitty O'Sullivan, New Zealand's modern grandmother. Auckland, Unity Press. 240p. *'A woman born to be loved of men.' Set in Australia and overseas.*

PARK, Rosina Ruth Lucia (Mrs D'Arcy Niland, wrote as Ruth Park). *Harp in the south.* Sydney, Angus & Robertson. 229p. Sequel *Poor man's orange, 1949.* *Set in the Sydney slum area of Surry Hills, the novel won first prize in the literary competition of the 'Sydney Morning Herald'.*

SCANLAN, Nelle. *The Rusty Road.* London, Hale. 307p. *Family life in a farming background.*

1949

BAUME, Eric. *Devil Lord's daughter.* Sydney, Invincible Press. 245p. *Partly based on Captain Cook's travels; Georgina Lord masquerades as a man.*

DAVIN, Daniel. *Roads from home.* London, Joseph. 254p. *Catholic families in Southland during the depression of the 1930s.*

DE MAUNY, Erik Cecil Leon. *The huntsman in his career.* London, Drummond. 263p. *Pacifist journalist, one of a party of soldiers assisting the police to track down a murderer. Based on the Graham case. See also R. M. Burdon's* Outlaw's progress, *1943.*

GUTHRIE, John. *Journey into twilight.* London, Laurie. 224p. *A novel about the publishing world in London.*

McDONALD, Georgina Bruce (Blaikie). *Grand hills for sheep.* Christchurch, Whitcombe & Tombs. 303p. *Scottish settlers in Otago mid-19th century. First prize 'Otago Daily Times' historical novel competition, 1948 centennial celebrations.*

MARSH, Ngaio. *Swing brother, swing.* London, Collins for the Crime Club. 299p. Published the same year in Boston by Little, Brown under the title *A wreath for Rivera.* *Disharmony in a dance band.*

PARK, Ruth. *Poor man's orange.* Sydney, Angus & Robertson. 276p. Sequel to *Harp in the south,* 1948. *Continues the story of the Darcy family with a special study of sixteen-year-old Dolour.*

QUENTIN, Dorothy. *The golden hibiscus.* London, Ward, Lock. 223p. *A romance in the world of entertainment.*

SARGESON, Frank. *I saw in my dream.* London, John Lehmann. 277p. The first part is *When the wind blows,* 1945. *Henry Griffiths is now David Spencer working on a farm, accepted by Maoris and searching for freedom.*

TEXIDOR, Greville (Mrs Droescher). *These dark glasses.* Christchurch, Caxton Press. 81p. *Told in diary form by Comrade Ruth Brown who visits friends in France who are writers and artists at the time of the Spanish civil war.*

1950

CARMAN, Dulce (Edith Marie Dulce Drummond). *The riddle of the ranges; a New Zealand romance.* London, Wright & Brown. 253p. *The mystery includes an adopted girl.*

CHERRILL, Amy Lilian. *Story of a New Zealand sheep farm.* Tunbridge Wells, Courier Printing and Publishing Company. 219p. *A London girl comes to New Zealand to marry a man she knows briefly and lives 'in the sticks'.*

COURAGE, James. *Desire without content.* London, Constable. 216p. *Study of a mother with an intellectually handicapped child, on a sheep station.*

GRIEVE, Mrs Hamilton. *It's nothing serious; a novel.* London, Museum Press. 220p. *A variety of people at a roadside teahouse twenty miles from Auckland.*

GUTHRIE, John. *Is this what I wanted?* London, Laurie. 252p. *A middle-aged lawyer in London just before World War II.*

GUTHRIE, John. *Merry-go-round.* London, Laurie. 240p. *Humorous treatment of an organisation similar to the British Council.*

PEACOCKE, Isabel. *Concerning the Marlows.* London, Ward, Lock. 224p. *Difficulties of a married couple who have a small son and separate.*

QUENTIN, Dorothy, pseudonym David King. *The mountains are still green.* London, Ward, Lock. 256p.
In 1836 a young couple leave England to join the man's uncle in Thames. Maning, Cowan and Baucke cited as references.

QUENTIN, Dorothy. *Reach me a star.* London, Ward, Lock. 255p.
Rosemary Combe is in the theatre in London with a company that later makes a tour around New Zealand.

SCANLAN, Nelle. *Confidence corner.* London, Hale. 318p.
Opposition by Manuka Bay residents when there is intention to use the Manuka Falls for fertiliser manufacture.

WHITWORTH, Jess. *Otago interval.* Hamilton, Paul's. 167p, illustrations.
The story of an Otago family starting from the gold rush era.

WILSON, Guthrie Edward Melville. *Brave company.* New York, Putnam. 246p.
A New Zealand infantry platoon in action in Italy in World War II.

1951

ANTHONY, Frank and Francis Jackson. *Me and Gus.* Illustrated by Neville Lodge. Wellington, Reed. 144p.
Based on revisions made for radio by Jackson on the dairy farm characters.

LAWSON, Will. *Gold in their hearts; a novel of New Zealand's early days.* Sydney, Invincible Press. 256p. Published in 1957 by Angus & Robertson under the title *Mary Smith's Hotel.*
Gold mining on the West Coast of the South Island.

MARSH, Ngaio. *Opening night.* London, Collins for the Crime Club. 255p. Published the same year in Boston by Little, Brown under the title *Night at the Vulcan.*
A young New Zealand actress is working at the Vulcan Theatre·when the first night produces a corpse.

PARK, Ruth. *The witch's thorn.* Sydney, Angus & Robertson. 220p.
Set in the King Country in the 1920s and 1930s. A sordid tale of poverty includes Maoris and Yugoslavs.

1952

ANTHONY, Frank and Francis Jackson. *More me and Gus.* Illustrated by Neville Lodge. Wellington, Reed. 144p.
Continues the series.

COURAGE, James. *Fires in the distance.* London, Constable. 288p.
Emotional problems of a family in the 1920s in Canterbury bush country.

EDEN, Dorothy. *Cat's prey.* London, Macdonald. 224p.
Mystery surrounds the visit of a woman to New Zealand where her aunt has died.

GILBERT, Gavin Robert. *Glass sharp and poisonous.* Christchurch, Caxton Press. 85p.
A nursing home in Europe whose patients are mainly rich elderly women.

GUTHRIE, John. *Paradise Bay.* London, Laurie. 254p.
The 75th anniversary of the arrival of immigrant ships at the Bay — New Plymouth.

GUTHRIE, John. *The seekers.* London, Laurie. 313p.
The first mate on a sailing ship comes to New Zealand and is killed fighting the Maoris. Maori background based on Elsdon Best. Filmed in England 1954.

RHODES, Denys. *Fly away Peter.* London, Richards Press. 258p.
A murder is planned.

SARGESON, Frank. *I for one.* Published in *Landfall* 22, June 1952. Published 1954, i.e. 1956?, by Caxton Press. 58p.
A spinster school teacher becomes interested in a visiting American psychologist.

SCANLAN, Nelle. *The young summer.* London, Hale. 320p.
A girl growing up in London with her conservative widowed father.

WILSON, Guthrie. *Julien Ware.* London, Hale. 287p.
Study of an ambitious life; farm, school, university and law.

1953

BAUME, Eric. *The mortal sin of Father Grossard.* Sydney, Angus & Robertson. 143p, illustrations.
After World War II an American woman goes to France to visit the grave of the son of a friend who has just died.

CATHIE, Diarmid Cameron, pseudonym. *She's right.* London, Collins. 191p.
An actor and producer from London leaves his family in the North Island to organise plays in the South Island.

EDEN, Dorothy. *Lamb to the slaughter*. London, Macdonald. 208p.
Mystery begins when a young woman comes to stay with a school teacher friend in the country.

FINLAYSON, Roderick. *The schooner came to Atia*. Auckland, Griffin Press. 1952, i.e. 1953. 144p.
Tragedy comes to a small group of people on a south sea island where a missionary is a main character.

HILL, Jean. *Wind may blow*. New Plymouth, printed by the Avery Press. 293p.
A religious novel of possessive and unpossessive love set in England during World War II; some links with New Zealand.

MARSH, Ngaio. *Spinsters in jeopardy*. Boston, Little, Brown. 278p. Published in London by Collins, 1954.
Alleyn is faced with some problems in France.

MASON, Henrietta Rex. *White orchid*. London, Longmans, Green. 276p.
'A New Zealand girl's experiences in the New Hebrides as governess to the children of a French-Polynesian marriage.' (Joan Stevens)

PARK, Ruth. *A power of roses*. Sydney, Angus & Robertson. 286p.
Teenager Miriam in a family story in Sydney.

QUENTIN, Dorothy. *The blue gum tree*. London, Ward, Lock. 189p.
A romance in a rural area.

SCOTT, Mary. *Breakfast at six*. London, Hurst & Blackett. 223p.
A city girl married to a sheep farmer.

1954

CAMPBELL, Margo. *The dark water*. London, A. Barker. 206p.
Life on a sheep station plus politics and a waterside workers' strike that made headlines.

CARMAN, Dulce. *The tapu tree; a romance of Maoriland*. London, Wright & Brown. 220p.
Love and hate in a mystery about the tapu tree.

COURAGE, James. *The young have secrets*. London, Cape. 270p.
The Garnett family in Sumner about 1914 where the bearded Mr Garnett runs a boys' preparatory school, as seen by ten-year-old Walter Blakiston.

EDEN, Dorothy. *Bride by candlelight*. London, Macdonald. 208p.
A woman is apprehensive about her fiancé she hasn't seen for some years when she rejoins him in New Zealand.

GARLAND, Stuart. *The importance of being honest*. Auckland, Oswald-Sealy. 208p.
Mystery, romance and humour with an impressionable young man and his friend, a private detective.

GILLIES, John Russell. *Voyagers in aspic*. London, Collins. 252p.
Comic treatment of New Zealanders with different backgrounds on a ship to England and in London.

McDONALD, Georgina. *Stinson's Bush; a novel*. Christchurch, Whitcombe & Tombs. 238p.
Rural life in the second half of the 19th century in an isolated part of Southland.

SCOTT, Mary. *Yours to oblige*. London, Hurst & Blackett. 223p.
A New Zealand romance.

WILSON, Guthrie. *The feared and the fearless*. London, Hale. 223p.
A study in violence of Captain Faulkner, known as Il Brutto and feared by enemy and ally in Italy in World War II.

1955

ANTHONY, Frank and Francis Jackson. *Me and Gus again;* illustrated by Neville Lodge. Wellington, Reed. 144p.
More humour about Gus and his cobber Mark.

CODY, Joseph Frederick. *The red kaka*. Wellington, Reed. 191p.
A convict escapes from Sydney in the early 19th century and is involved in Maori tribal wars.

JEFFERY, Margaret. *The forsaken orchard*. London, Hale. 192p.
A family on a fruit farm and a girl growing up. Based on the author's radio serial 1953.

KENYON, Frank Wilson. *Emma*. London, Hutchinson. 380p.
A novel about Lady Hamilton and Lord Nelson.

MACKERSEY, Ian. *Crusader Fox King*. London, Hale. 189p.
An aircraft flying from Australia to New Zealand suffers alarming damage.

MANN, Catherine. *The silent mountain*. London, Wright & Brown. 188p.
In the late 19th century a seven-year-old European girl is kidnapped by an old Maori woman in retaliation against pakehas.

MARSH, Ngaio. *Scales of justice*. London, Collins for the Crime Club. 255p, plan on linings.
A corpse is discovered near a stream where there is local interest in catching an enormous trout.

PARK, Ruth. *Pink flannel*. Illustrated by Phil Taylor. Sydney, Angus & Robertson. 223p.
Humorous story told by Jenny, an orphan from Australia who comes to a New Zealand country town to live with her four aunts.

PHIPPS, Grace Mary (Palk). *Marriage with Eve.* Wellington, Reed. 192p.
A family tale told with some humour.

QUENTIN, Dorothy. *The generous heart.* London, Ward, Lock. 188p.
Set in New Zealand and the Pacific.

SANDFORD, Kenneth Leslie. *Dead reckoning.* London, Hutchinson. 207p.
A thriller in which Maxim Hale a solicitor is up against some tough characters in the Waikato and Coromandel.

WILLS, Cecil Melville. *Death in the dark.* London, Hutchinson. 192p.
Two detectives in New Zealand, apparently on vacation, are soon investigating crime.

WILSON, Helen. *Land of my children.* Hamilton, Paul. xv, 214p.
Farming life covering two generations, with a touch of humour.

WINDER, Mavis Areta (Wright). *Shadowed journey.* London, Jenkins. 191p.
Based on the Tangiwai train disaster of Christmas Eve 1953.

WINGATE, March. *Red East.* London, Herbert Jenkins. 190p.
Two girls at school together in a rural area and later working in the city in love with the same man.

1956

COURAGE, James. *The call home.* London, Cape. 252p.
Following the death of his wife in the 1930s, Norman Grant returns to the family farm, the scene of his childhood, fifty miles from Christchurch.

CRISP, Frank. *Maori Jack's monster.* London, Hodder & Stoughton. 190p.
The log of a brig dated 1849 records mysterious disappearances of people on the ship.

DAVIN, Dan. *The sullen bell.* London, Joseph. 287p.
A former officer of the New Zealand Division in the Middle East during World War II now in London after the war. Hugh a portrait of the author.

DORIEN, Ray. *Flower of delight.* London, W. H. Allen. 191p.
A young woman is a companion to an elderly spinster seeking in New Zealand a man she wouldn't marry thirty years before.

HILL, Jean O'Hagan (Morton). *Sun at noon.* London, Herbert Jenkins. 192p.
A minister of religion works hard for others, to the detriment of his family.

JONES, Arthur Edwin. *You know the way it is, a Felix Holliday story.* London, Hutchinson. 208p.
Holliday is asked to trace a missing girl.

McCARTHY, Darry. *Fly away dove!* London, Joseph. 271p.
Love story of an English girl in Italy.

McCLYMONT, Margot Kate. *The dark valley.* London, Wright & Brown. 190p.
A man marries a woman for her money.

MANN, Catherine. *One who bears your name.* London, Wright & Brown. 191p.
A man is vexed when his son marries a part-Maori girl.

MARSH, Ngaio. *Death of a fool.* Boston, Little, Brown. 302p. Published in London by Collins, 1957, under the title *Off with his head.*
Based on ritual dancing in England.

PHIPPS, Grace. *The women of the family.* Wellington, Reed. 188p.
Family tale where there are two daughters, one married.

PRESTON, Florence Margaret. *A gallows tree.* London, Cassell. 254p.
A woman's unhappy marriage.

REES, Rosemary. *Better to trust...* London, Chapman & Hall. 272p.
Linda Parbury in England and later on a New Zealand sheep station.

REYBURN, Wallace. *Follow a shadow.* London, Cassell. 215p.
A young woman on a ship from London to New York and in love with the captain; a gale endangers the ship and makes world news. Prompted by the 'Flying Enterprise' sinking of 1952.

SCOTT, Mary. *Families are fun.* Auckland, Paul's Book Arcade. 218p.
A story of the sisters Freddie and Angela.

THWAITES, Frederick Joseph. *That was the hour.* Sydney, Edwards. 286p.
A semi-historical novel of a doctor who comes to New Zealand and is living near Mt Tarawera prior to the eruption of 1886.

WILSON, Guthrie. *Sweet white wine.* London, Hale. 220p.
Simon Gregg at 51 is a successful novelist. The author was successful in a libel action over a review in 'The Times' of Palmerston North, 22 September 1956.

WINDER, Mavis. *The stubble field.* Wellington, Reed. 192p.
A widow marries a man who has an adopted daughter.

YAGER, Marie J. *Complex counterpart.* Pageant Press. 218p.
Set in late 19th century Spain, the novel is about two women, one an actress, of similar appearance but different temperament.

1957

BURFIELD, Eva, pseudonym of Mrs Frances Eva Ebbett. *Yellow kowhai.* London, Wright & Brown. 191p.
A young woman leaves England for New Zealand to marry a middle-aged widower.

CROSS, Ian. *The God boy.* New York, Harcourt, Bruce & Co. 184p.
The study of a rebellious boy with a Catholic background.

ELLIS, Michael, pseudonym of Stephen Peter Llewellyn. *The score at tea-time.* London, Peter Davies. 287p.
New Zealanders in the Korean war.

FENTON, Elizabeth. *Beware my heart; a New Zealand romance.* London, Hale. 192p.
A farmer invites an English woman to come to New Zealand and marry him.

FRAME, Janet Paterson. *Owls do cry.* Christchurch, Pegasus Press. 210p. Sequels *Faces in the water,* 1961 and *The edge of the alphabet,* 1962.
The Withers family of three girls and a boy grow up; twenty years later one girl is in a mental hospital.

JOSEPH, George Israel. *Lie fallow my acre.* Wellington, Reed. 187p.
A woman is married to an American who discriminates against Maoris.

LORD, Albert Fawcett. *Kauri Hill.* Wellington, Reed. 176p.
Farming background in North Auckland; romance and tapu.

PARK, Ruth. *One-a-pecker, two-a-pecker.* Sydney, Angus & Robertson. 232p. Published as a Pan paperback in 1962 under the title *The frost and the fire.*
Currency MacQueen, a girl of eighteen, and the Otago gold rush days of 1863.

PRESTON, Florence. *Harvest of daring.* London, Cassell. 256p.
A story of two girl cousins, one with a farming background, the other from the city.

REYBURN, Wallace. *Port of Call.* London, Cassell. 191p.
A thriller about a man who needs money in a hurry and has the opportunity to pick up £5000 for an undisclosed job.

SALTER, Elizabeth. *Death in a mist.* London, Bles. 254p.
Death at a tourist resort.

SCOTT, Mary. *The unwritten book.* Wellington, Reed. 252p.
Family and farm can cause inconvenient interruptions to an aspiring novelist.

WILSON, Guthrie. *Strip Jack naked.* London, Hale. 157p.
Jack Stevens, an Englishman, deserts his ship in Wellington and gets into trouble ashore.

1958

ASHTON-WARNER, Sylvia Constance (Mrs Henderson). *Spinster.* London, Secker & Warburg. 269p.
An unorthodox teacher with Maori children in a country school. Filmed in the United States in 1961 under the title Two loves.

BOSWELL, John. *The Blue Pheasant.* London, Collins. 256p.
Crime in Hong Kong and New Zealand; the title is the name of a Hong Kong nightclub.

BURFIELD, Eva, pseudonym. *A chair to sit on.* London, Wright & Brown. 188p.
People in a guest house in sunny Napier.

CAMERON, Ian. *The midnight sea.* London, Hutchinson. 199p.
Convoy ships to Russia in World War II and the Fleet Air Arm.

FRANCE, Helena Ruth. *The race.* London, Constable. 191p.
A yacht race between Wellington and Lyttleton provides the opportunity to examine those on the yachts and people on land who are personally involved.

GURR, Thomas Stuart and H. H. Cox. *Obsession.* London, Muller. 254p.
A semi-documentary treatment of a 1954 murder case trial against two teenage girls, one the daughter of the victim.

JOSEPH, Michael Kennedy. *I'll soldier no more.* London, Gollancz. 272p.
Character studies of soldiers, British and a New Zealander, after the Normandy invasion in 1944.

McCLYMONT, Margot. *Green harmony.* London, Wright & Brown. 190p.
The story of a doctor in love.

MANNING, Arthur. *We never die in winter.* London, Jenkins. 191p.
Four men and three women trapped in a bus in a tunnel by a landslide.

MARSH, Ngaio. *Singing in the shrouds.* London, Collins for the Crime Club. 255p.
When a death is reported as a ship leaves London for South Africa, Alleyn boards the vessel at Portsmouth.

MESSENGER, Elizabeth, i.e. Betty Margery (Esson). *Murder stalks the bay.* London, Hale. 191p.
An unhappy introduction to New Zealand for a recent arrival from England.

NOONAN, Michael. *The patchwork hero.* London, Heinemann. 254p. Sequel *The December boys,* 1958.
A roistering tugboat captain in Australia.

PRESTON, Florence. *Great refusals.* London, Cassell. 246p.
Continues the story of Harvest of daring, *1957, with Kathrine and her daughter Judy.*

REES, Rosemary. *Love is a lonely land.* London, Harrap. 223p.
A New Zealand 19th century romance.

RUHEN, Olaf. *Naked under Capricorn.* London, Macdonald. 254p.
A white man has contact with aborigines in the Australian desert.

SUTTON, Phyllis. *Marana.* London, W. H. Allen. 207p.
A New Zealand romance about a girl who arrives from England to marry and discovers she has been jilted.

1959

BRATHWAITE, Errol Freeman. *Fear in the night.* Christchurch, Caxton Press. 165p.
An aircraft makes a forced landing in Japanese territory during World War II.

COURAGE, James. *A way of love.* London, Cape. 255p.
A homosexual relationship in London. The novel was banned in New Zealand.

DAVIN, Daniel. *No remittance.* London, Joseph. 223p.
A young Protestant architect from England marries into an Irish Catholic family in Southland.

DUCKWORTH, Marilyn Rose (Adcock). *A gap in the spectrum.* London, Hutchinson. 191p.
Frieda, a part-time university student, in love with a shiftless man.

FOWLER, Percy Leo. *Brown conflict; a tale of white man and Maori, 1861-2.* Wellington, Reed. 267p, map.
A young man in commerce, a friend of the Maoris; includes Gorst, Fox and Rewi Maniopoto.

LINDSAY, Kathleen. *Beware of the dawn.* London, Hurst & Blackett. 199p.
A woman condemned to death in England escapes to New Zealand in the 1840s.

MARSH, Ngaio. *False scent.* Boston, Little Brown. 273p. English edition Collins, 1960.
A theatre birthday party results in work for the undertaker.

MESSENGER, Elizabeth. *Material witness.* London, Hale. 175p.
When he arrives at his fishing lodge in Taupo, the owner discovers a dead girl.

PRESTON, Florence. *The gay pretensions.* London, Cassell. 247p.
A girl with an unfortunate background comes before the court and is sentenced to Borstal training.

QUENTIN, Dorothy. *The unchanging love.* London, Ward, Lock. 191p.
Doctor, nurse romance in a small New Zealand town.

ST. BRUNO, Albert Francis, wrote as Frank Bruno. *The hellbuster.* London, Hale. 204p.
Set in the Bay of Islands (the 'Hell of the Pacific') where a ship drops anchor, Christmas 1843.

SCOTT, Mary. *The White Elephant.* Hamilton, Paul's Book Arcade. 201p.
Life in a guest house by the sea run by two women.

SLATTER, Gordon Cyril. *A gun in my hand.* Christchurch, Pegasus Press. 239p.
A psychological study of an ex-serviceman suffering from war neurosis.

STRINGFELLOW, Mrs Olga. *The fresh and the salt.* Toronto, Doubleday. 384p. Published in London by Collins, 1960, under the title *Mary Bravender.*
Experiences of a 21-year-old Scottish emigrant woman who arrives in New Zealand in 1862.

SUMMERS, Essie. *The lark in the meadow*. London, Mills & Boon. Published in the 'Woman's Weekly Library', no. 184, under the title *The long journey*.
A nurse leaves London for New Zealand.

TINDALE, Norman Barnett and Harold A. Lindsay. *Rangatira, the high-born; a Polynesian saga*. Illustrated by Douglas F. Maxted. Wellington, Reed. 208p. Background and notes pp183-208.
The Australian authors describe the lives of thirty Polynesians who desert their cramped island home in the 14th century and make the voyage to New Zealand.

WILSON, Guthrie. *Dear Miranda*. London, Hutchinson. 223p.
Australian-born Miranda and the various men in her life through marriage and divorce. Set in Australia and England.

1960

ASHTON-WARNER, Sylvia. *Incense to idols*. London, Secker & Warburg. 283p.
A Parisian exile in New Zealand, Germaine de Beauvais, concert pianist, tells of the men close to her.

CARELL, Victor. *Naked we are born*. Sydney, Ure Smith. 227p.
The impact of white civilisation on the cultures of Papuans, Australian aboriginals and Maoris. 'Islands of the white clouds' (the Maori section) pp167-227.

CROSS, Ian. *The backward sex*. London, Deutsch. 191p.
Young Robbie Henderson tells the story of his adolescence and the dominating and provocative Mrs Rainer.

CRUMP, Barry John. *A good keen man*. Illustrated by Dennis Turner. Wellington, Reed. 192p.
Humorous account of experiences while deer culling.

DAVIS, Thomas and Lydia Davis. *Makutu*. London, Joseph. 239p.
Makutu, or willing a person to death, is used by Cook Islanders against an interfering American spinster.

DEVERELL, Dijon (Evangeline). *Recognition*. New York, Pageant Press. 234p.
Historical novel on Captain William Dampier, 1652-1715, 'the true discoverer of Terra Australis'.

DUCKWORTH, Marilyn. *The match-box house*. London, Hutchinson. 190p.
A woman accepts as boarders three children whose mother is in hospital but the task is too much for her.

EDEN, Dorothy. *Sleep in the woods*. London, Hodder & Stoughton. 284p.
Pioneer life in 19th century New Zealand includes trouble with the Hauhaus.

HILLIARD, Noel Harvey. *Maori girl*. London, Heinemann. 263p. Sequels are: *Power of joy*, 1965, *Maori woman*, 1974 and *The glory and the dream*, 1978.
Netta Samuel leaves her derelict home in Taranaki to work as a housemaid in Wellington and soon becomes familiar with the worst aspects of city life.

KEINZLY, Mrs Frances, pseudonym? *Tangahano*. London, P. Davies. 254p.
A couple and their youngsters leave the comfort of Auckland to make big money at a new dam construction job in the Waikato.

LLEWELLYN, Stephen, pseudonym Michael Ellis. *The angel in the coffin*. London, P. Davies. 249p.
A middle-aged bachelor is the chief character on a Dutch ship bringing people to New Zealand.

MANNING, Arthur. *The short madness*. London, Hale. 191p.
Conflict between two men, one an Australian, in a small coastal town.

MASON, Henrietta Rex. *Fool's gold*. London, Hale. 192p. Sequel *Our hills cry woe!* 1963.
Narrated in the first person from the diary of a girl of seventeen who arrives at Hokitika in 1865 and goes ashore disguised as a man.

MESSENGER, Elizabeth. *Light on murder*. London, Hale. 191p.
Mystery, death and a lighthouse.

MUIR, Macgregor Robin. *Word for word*. Christchurch, Pegasus. 287p.
Humorous account of the publishing business. A young woman writes a novel that could be a best seller.

PRESTON, Ivy Alice (Kinross). *Where ratas twine*. London, Wright & Brown. 176p.
When her widowed father remarries, Dawn Calder leaves Stewart Island to live on the mainland.

QUENTIN, Dorothy. *Rainbow Valley*. London, Ward, Lock. 190p.
Life in a small town south of Auckland.

REYBURN, Wallace. *Three women*. London, Cassell. 185p.
Mystery story set in London and at sea.

RHODES, Denys. *The syndicate*. London, Longmans, Green. 275p, map.
The search for uranium in East Africa is big business.

ROGERS, Ray Mount. *The Long White Cloud.*
Christchurch, Whitcombe & Tombs. 346p.
*An ex-convict from England goes to New Zealand
and is determined to train a horse to win the English
Grand National Steeplechase.*

RUHEN, Olaf. *White man's shoes.* London,
Macdonald. 240p.
*European influences on a Pacific island after World
War II and the vices of a local leader create problems
for the Australian administrator.*

ST. BRUNO, Francis. *Black noon at Ngutu.* London,
Hale. 189p.
Taranaki wars 1868 given blood-curdling treatment.

SCOTT, Mary and Joyce West. *Fatal lady.* Hamilton,
Paul's Book Arcade. 204p.
*When a man is found dead in a paddock his racehorse
is suspected.*

SCOTT, Mary. *No sad songs.* Auckland, Paul's Book
Arcade. 218p.
Freddie and her sister in the country.

WILSON, Guthrie. *The incorruptibles.* London,
Hutchinson. 199p.
*The selection of a headmaster for a boys' secondary
school in Sydney provides the author with the
opportunity of examining the candidates.*

1961

BOOTH, Patrick. *Long night among the stars.* London,
Collins. 191p.
*A prizewinner in the 'Otago Daily Times' centennial
competition. The background and preparations for the
first Briton to accomplish space travel; set mainly in
Australia but includes New Zealand.*

BRATHWAITE, Errol. *An affair of men.* London,
Collins, and the 'Otago Daily Times', Dunedin.
254p.
*Winner of the 'Otago Daily Times' centennial
competition. Conflict between Japanese violence and
Christian pacifism in World War II on Bougainville.*

BRENT, Marama. *Bird in the wilderness.* London,
Hale; Christchurch, Whitcombe & Tombs. 191p.
*Patience Mortimer, a university graduate, takes a
vacation job in the Bay of Islands and soon marries.*

COURAGE, James. *The visit to Penmorten.* London,
Cape. 222p.
*A young man goes to Cornwall for a holiday and meets
a psychoanalyst.*

CROSS, Ian. *After Anzac Day.* London, Deutsch.
235p.
*A civil servant and his wife take into their home an
expectant unmarried mother; a study of the people
in the household and aspects of New Zealand life.*

CRUMP, Barry John. *Hang on a minute mate.*
Wellington, Reed. 192p. Illustrated by Dennis
Turner.
*Humour with Sam Cash and his mate in a variety of
jobs and incidents.*

FRAME, Janet. *Faces in the water.* Christchurch,
Pegasus Press. 219p. Preceded by *Owls do cry*, 1957.
Sequel *The edge of the alphabet*, 1962.
*A young woman recounts her several years spent in
two mental hospitals. The author has said that it is
her only work she would label autobiographical; a
London doctor had suggested she write her experiences
as an exercise in therapy.*

FRANCE, Mrs Helena Ruth. *Ice cold river.* London,
Constable. 257p.
*A family gathering at Christmas at the farm on the
banks of the flooding Waimakariri River.*

GARFORD, James. *Seventeen come Sunday.* London,
Faber. 253p.
*A boy growing up before, during and after World
War II.*

GRIFFIN, Andrew Dow. *Sailin' down the Clyde.*
Auckland, Business Printing Works. 223p.
*The story of Terence Drummond at sea on different
ships.*

KENYON, Frank. *Mrs Nelly* or *Restoration
divertimento; being a story based on the life and
adventures of one Eleanor Gwyn, server of strong
waters, orange girl, actress, lady of pleasure and royal
mistress.* London, Hutchinson. 252p.
Nell Gwynn and King Charles II.

MACKENZIE, Andrew. *Voice from the cell.* London,
Hale. 192p.
*A journalist becomes involved in the underworld and
the mistress of a criminal.*

PARK, Ruth. *The good-looking women.* Sydney, Angus
& Robertson. 243p.
*Study of adults and children of a Catholic family in
Sydney.*

1962

CARMAN, Dulce. *The false dawn (a romance of
Maori land).* London, Wright & Brown. 176p.
*A scientist whose life is abruptly changed for the worse,
is helped by a Maori friend.*

CARMAN, Dulce. *The miracle of Tane.* London,
Wright & Brown. 208p.
Marriage difficulties between Maori and Pakeha.

CRUMP, Barry. *One of us.* Illustrated by Dennis
Turner. Wellington, Reed. 181p.
*Sam Cash and his shiftless mates are loath to accept
regular employment.*

DAVIS, Michael Henry Lester. *Mutton on the menu.* Illustrated by Keith S. Clark. Wellington, Reed. 192p.
Farming and Maori neighbours.

EDEN, Dorothy. *Whistle for the crows.* London, Hodder & Stoughton. 221p.
A sinister tale set in Ireland.

FRAME, Janet. *The edge of the alphabet.* Christchurch, Pegasus Press. 224p.
The last of the trilogy on the Withers family. Toby an epileptic meets on the ship to England a spinster school teacher and a bus driver and they meet again in London. 'The edge of the alphabet where words crumble and all form of communication between the living are useless. One day we who live at the edge of the alphabet will find our speech.'

GEE, Maurice Gough. *The big season.* London, Hutchinson. 198p.
Life in a small town has problems for a young, popular rugby football player who has several other interests.

GRAYLAND, Valerie Merle (Spanner). *The dead men of Eden.* London, Hale; Christchurch, Whitcombe & Tombs. 188p.
Eighteen-year-old Julia and her brother in the gold fields at Thames in the 1880s.

JOSEPH, George Israel. *When the rainbow is pale.* London, Hale; Christchurch, Whitcombe & Tombs. 192p.
An English sailor among the Maoris in the early 19th century.

JOSEPH, Michael Kennedy. *A pound of saffron.* London, Gollancz; Hamilton, Paul. 253p.
James Rankin, Professor of European Drama at the University of Auckland, has ambitions towards a major Unesco post but despite his Machiavellian methods there are obstacles.

MARSH, Ngaio. *Hand in glove.* London, Collins for the Crime Club. 256p.
Fox and Alleyn arrive in an English village to probe into a violent death.

MESSENGER, Elizabeth. *Golden dawns the sun.* London, Hale. 191p.
Life for a girl in the Otago goldfields complicated with three men in love with her.

PHIPPS, Grace. *The young wife.* London, Jenkins. 176p.
A young woman is married to a man twice her age.

PRESTON, Ivy. *Magic in Maoriland.* London, Wright & Brown. 172p.
A girl from England becomes engaged to a half-caste Maori.

REES, Rosemary. *The proud Diana.* London, Wright & Brown; Christchurch, Whitcombe & Tombs. 174p.
A young woman from England has problems on a sheep station partly because of her attitude to Maoris.

REYBURN, Wallis. *Good and evil.* London, Cassell. 207p.
A woman and her sex life in England and abroad.

ST. BRUNO, Francis. *Fury at Finnegan's Folly.* London, Hale. 186p.
The tough life of the goldfields on the West Coast of the South Island in the 1860s.

SANDERSON, Nora (Brocas). *Hospital in New Zealand.* London, Mills & Boon. 188p.
A romance which includes some curious individuals.

SCOTT, Mary and Joyce West. *Such nice people.* Hamilton, Paul's Book Arcade; Sydney, Angus & Robertson. 174p.
A murder is committed and several people come under suspicion.

SMITH, Michael L. *No easy answer.* London, Hutchinson. 223p.
An Oxford undergraduate and his problems.

TULLETT, James Stuart. *Tar White.* London, Hale. 191p.
Life on New Zealand whaling stations in the 1840s, based on historical fact.

WALLIS, Redmond Frankton. *Point of origin.* London, Bodley Head. 207p.
Love affair between a salesman in Christchurch and a university student.

WINDER, Mavis. *Memory's yoke.* London, Wright & Brown. 174p.
A girl in love with a new arrival from England.

WORBOYS, Anne (Eyre). *Call from a stranger.* London, Ward, Lock. 187p.
A woman learns of her husband's earlier marriage.

WORBOYS, Anne. *Three strings to a fortune.* London, Hurst & Blackett. 183p.
A girl stands to inherit some money provided she marries one of the sons of the deceased.

1963

ADDISON, Mrs Doris Maureen (Bentley). *Valley in the clouds.* London, Hale; Christchurch, Whitcombe & Tombs. 190p.
A sole-charge school teacher and his wife in an isolated North Island community.

ADSETT, Delphin Rose (wrote as Dell Adsett). *A magpie sings.* Wellington, Price Milburn. 221p.
A farming area from the turn of the century to World War I.

ANTHONY, Frank and Francis Jackson. *The complete me and Gus.* Illustrated by Neville Lodge. Wellington, Reed. 431p. Contains *Me and Gus* (1951), *More me and Gus* (1952), *Me and Gus again* (1955).
Humorous treatment of life in a rural area.

ARCHIBALD, Menie. *The long white cloud.* Ilfracombe, Stockwell. 320p.
'The selfishness and irresponsibility of a beautiful girl casts a shadow over three generations.'

AUDLEY, Ernest Henry. *No boots for Mr Moehau.* London, Hodder & Stoughton. 189p.
A small Maori population on the Coromandel Peninsula.

BACON, Ronald Leonard. *In the sticks.* Illustrations by David More. London, Collins. 184p.
Largely humorous account of teaching in a sole-charge school by an inexperienced headmaster.

BALLANTYNE, David. *The last pioneer.* London, Hale. 191p.
A Londoner arrives with his young son in a small New Zealand town and is soon part of the community and facing problems.

BENNETT, Margot. *That summer's earthquake.* London, Eyre & Spottiswoode, 1963, i.e. 1964? 253p.
The author, an English woman, makes use of her 18 months in New Zealand in the 1930s; her story includes sheep farming and the Napier earthquake of 1931.

BROWN, J. Edward. *Luck of the islands.* Illustrated by Keith S. Clark. Wellington, Reed. 191p.
A Rarotongan family wins £12 000 in a New Zealand lottery and comes to that country.

CARMAN, Dulce. *The Maori gateway; a romance of Maoriland.* London, Wright & Brown. 173p.
A romance with a Maori background.

CASEY, R. (pseudonym of Kenneth Robert Christian). *As short a spring.* Hamilton, Paul. 296p.
After trying several jobs, 21-year-old John Hill goes to university intending to become a teacher. A farmer's daughter the chief female character.

CRUMP, Barry. *There and back.* Illustrated by Dennis Turner. Wellington, Reed. 187p.
Humorous adventures of Sam Cash.

DINGWELL, Joyce. *The New Zealander.* London, Mills & Boon. 192p.
An Australian girl finds romance in New Zealand.

DUCKWORTH, Marilyn. *A barbarous tongue.* London, Hutchinson. 188p.
The first-person narrative of Frieda, a part-time student in love.

EDEN, Dorothy. *The bird in the chimney.* London, Hodder & Stoughton. 255p.
A girl living with rich relations in 19th century England.

FRAME, Janet. *Scented gardens for the blind.* Christchurch, Pegasus Press. 192p.
Husband, wife and daughter have problems of communication. 'Why can't you speak? Why don't we just sit down together like ordinary people and speak?'

GRAYLAND, Valerie. *Night of the reaper.* London, Hale; Christchurch, Whitcombe & Tombs. 192p.
Mystery story in Northland with a Maori sleuth.

HARVEY, Norman Bruce. *Any old dollars Mister?* Hamilton, Paul. 155p.
Humorous account of two eleven-year-olds in Wellington scrounging from the Americans during World War II.

HILL, Jean. *A family affair.* London, John Gresham. 160p.
A widow and her daughter leave New Zealand to visit people in England.

HUGHES, Ivy. *The singing water.* London, Hale; Christchurch, Whitcombe & Tombs. 185p.
New Zealand in the 1850s. The characters include a missionary and a Maori chief.

HURNE, Ralph. *Larks in cages.* London, Alvin Redman. 254p.
Scenes of army life in England; and set partly in New Zealand.

JOSEPH, George. *The insider.* London, Boardman. 143p.
Thriller about a professional killer after a police witness.

JOYCE, Thomas Heath. *Whose candle is the sun.* London, Abelard-Schuman. 330p, map.
English settlers and Spaniards on an island in the West Indies in the 17th century.

KENNEDY, Marion. *The wrong side of the door.* London, Harrap. 285p.
A trainee nurse at a New Zealand mental hospital. Fiction or non-fiction?

MACKAY, Mrs Margaret Elizabeth. *Amanda.* Christchurch, Whitcombe & Tombs. 322p.
A farming community in the South Island in the 1890s.

MADDOCK, Shirley Francis Whitley. *With gently smiling jaws.* Auckland, Collins. 228p.
Light-hearted tale of a girl in her early twenties who leaves New Zealand for New York and works in commercial television.

MANNING, Arthur. *Tainted money.* London, Hale. 191p.
Topdressing pilots, Blenheim and the Sounds and £10 000.

MASON, Henrietta. *Our hills cry woe!* Christchurch, Whitcombe & Tombs. 207p. Second of a trilogy: *Fool's gold* (1960); *High acres* (1966).
High country sheep station; Roger Spencer farmer, lawyer and member of parliament.

MESSENGER, Elizabeth. *A heap of trouble.* London, Hale. 191p.
A detective story set in the Bay of Islands.

MORRIESON, James Ronald Hugh. *The scarecrow; a novel.* Sydney, Angus & Robertson. 211p.
Small New Zealand town as seen by a fourteen-year-old boy; the scarecrow is a sex maniac.

NOONAN, Michael. *The December boys.* London, Heinemann. 191p. Sequel to *The patchwork hero.*
Some boys from a Catholic orphanage meet eccentric people in a district by the sea.

PEARSON, Bill, i.e. William Harrison Pearson. *Coal Flat.* Auckland, Paul. 421p.
A young teacher Paul Rogers returns to Coal Flat on the West Coast of the South Island after service in the army. Comprehensive study of the people and the town which could be Greymouth where the author was born.

PETERS, Charles, pseudonym Charles Francis. *The big one.* Christchurch, Whitcombe & Tombs. 203p.
Hunting crocodiles in Australia.

PHIPPS, Grace. *A nurse like Kate.* London, Jenkins. 175p.
A doctor-and-nurse romance at a Christchurch hospital.

PRESTON, Ivy. *Island of enchantment.* London, Hale. 189p.
Romance at Stewart Island and Dunedin.

PRESTON, Ivy. *Tamarask in bloom.* London, Hale; Christchurch, Whitcombe & Tombs. 190p.
A girl and her love problems.

QUENTIN, Dorothy. *The dark castle.* London, Ward, Lock. 190p.
A hospital romance set in Italy.

ST. BRUNO, Francis. *Cockeye Kerrigan.* London, Hale. 190p.
Boxing in Australia.

ST. BRUNO, Francis. *Yellow Jack's island.* London, Hale. 192p.
Rugged adventures in the Pacific in the 19th century.

SANDERSON, Nora. *The ordeal of Nurse Thompson.* London, Mills & Boon. 189p.
A jealous nurse and another with a loss of memory.

SANDERSON, Nora. *The two faces of Nurse Roberts.* London, Mills & Boon. 188p.
A girl takes up nursing at a hospital where she knows a doctor.

SCOTT, Mary. *The long honeymoon.* Hamilton, Paul. 201p.
Over the summer holidays at their seaside farm, a newly-married couple have a number of visitors.

SCOTT, Mary and Joyce West. *The mangrove murder.* Auckland, Paul. 176p.
A jilted girl finds the body of a man in a boat.

STEPHENSON, Ralph. *Body in my arms.* London, John Gifford. 190p.
A radio announcer in Auckland discovers the body of a dead girl.

SUMMERS, Essie. *South to forget.* London, Mills & Boon. 189p.
A young man rejected by his girl asks another to pose as his fiancee.

SUMMERS, Essie. *Where no roads go.* London, Mills & Boon. 190p.
Hostility between a man and a woman who inherit a guest house.

THOMAS, William Herne. *The man who gave.* Auckland, Printed by Clark & Matheson. 172p.
A man wants the thrill of giving money away to people who need it.

TULLETT, James. *Yellow streak.* London, Hale; Christchurch, Whitcombe & Tombs. 190p.
Present-day prospecting for gold and the conflicts of the people involved.

WILSON, Guthrie. *The return of the snow-white puritan,* by John Paolotti, pseudonym. London, Cassell. 227p.
An American returns to Italy to seek a girl he knew twenty years earlier during World War II.

WILSON, Phillip John. *Beneath the thunder.* London, Hale. 188p.
Some marital discord in a farming community of pakeha and Maori in the Waikato.

WINDER, Mavis. *How great a fire.* London, Wright
& Brown. 174p.
Did the girl want to marry the man for his money?

1964

ADDISON, Doris. *Mara.* London, Hale; Christchurch, Whitcombe & Tombs. 192p.
*Begins shortly before World War I when a Maori girl
marries a school teacher. Problems of race also affect
their descendants.*

ASHTON-WARNER, Sylvia. *Bell call.* New York,
Simon & Schuster. 317p.
*Tarl Prackett wants freedom for herself and her
children. 'We don't send our children to school until
they want to go. The symbiosis between mother and
child should not be broken until the child himself
breaks it.'*

BACON, Ronald. *Along the road.* Illustrations by
David More. Auckland, Collins. 186p. Sequel to
In the sticks, 1963.
*The sole-charge teacher now has an assistant, Rachel
Brooks. Some race problems.*

BENJAMIN, Philip. *Quick before it melts.* London,
Gollancz. 247p.
*A United States journalist in Christchurch and
Antarctica, told with some humour.*

BOOTH, Pat. *Footsteps in the sea.* Auckland, Collins.
256p.
*The New Zealand way of life in a small town and
Japanese fishing offshore as seen by a man after a
a ten-year absence.*

BRATHWAITE, Errol. *The flying fish.* Auckland,
Collins. 383p, 2 maps. Sequel *The needle's eye,* 1965.
*The Maori wars in Taranaki, characters and
conflicts 1860-61.*

BRATHWAITE, Errol. *Long way home.* Christchurch, Caxton Press. 189p.
*Rescue operations following an RNZAF plane crash in
the South Island.*

BURFIELD, Eva. *The long winter.* London, Wright
& Brown. 176p.
A befriended hitch hiker comes under suspicion.

BURGESS, Michael. *Mister.* Introduction by Robert
Allerton. London, Hutchinson New Authors. 181p.
*Episodic narrative of life in a New Zealand prison
where an officer is known as 'Himmler'. Documentary
fiction.*

CARMAN, Dulce. *The pool of wisdom.* London,
Wright & Brown. 172p.
A romance with a slight Maori background.

CARMAN, Dulce. *Tomorrow's sun.* London, Wright
& Brown. 175p.
*A woman worried because her soldier husband missing
in Malaya.*

CLARKE, Mrs Neva Yvonne. *Behind closed doors.*
London, Hale; Christchurch, Whitcombe & Tombs.
176p.
Neighbouring families and the hostility among them.

COOP, Harold Valentine, wrote as Harold Valentine.
House surgeon. Christchurch, Whitcombe & Tombs.
174p.
A newly-qualified doctor working in a public hospital.

COOPER, Mrs Evelyn Barbara. *Target for malice.*
London, Hale; Christchurch, Whitcombe & Tombs.
188p.
*A small isolated community which attracts the
attention of the police.*

CRUMP, Barry. *Gulf.* Illustrated by Will Mahony.
Wellington, Reed. 172p.
*Set in the Gulf of Carpentaria, Australia and based
on the author's experiences as a professional crocodile
hunter.*

CRUMP, Walter William. *McDunnit dunnit.*
Auckland, Ace Distributors. 176p.
*Humorous tale of farm life. The author is the father
of Barry Crump.*

DAVIS, Michael Henry Lester. *Watersiders.*
Wellington, Reed. 174p.
*Reminiscences of life on the waterfront, the dangers
and the perks associated with it.*

EDEN, Dorothy. *Bella.* London, Hodder &
Stoughton. 253p.
Mystery and melodrama in Victorian London.

FENWICK, Margaret. *The tempered wind.* London,
Hale; Christchurch, Whitcombe & Tombs. 176p.
*A woman leaves England to begin a fresh life in
New Zealand but is soon faced with problems.*

GEDDES, Adrienne Marie (Kelliher). *The rim of
eternity.* Auckland, Collins. 175p.
*Science fiction with an invasion of New Zealand from
another planet.*

GEE, Wallace. *Moral issues here and abroad.*
Ilfracombe, Stockwell. 304p.
*Farming in New Zealand with the addition of
considerable propaganda.*

GRAYLAND, Valerie. *The grave-digger's apprentice.*
Christchurch, Whitcombe & Tombs. 192p.
Further crime with the Maori detective in Auckland.

HENSHAW, William Keith. *Kath.* London, Collins.
256p.
A corpse is discovered in a church under construction.

HOUSE, L. C. (Lesley), pseudonym of Elsie Macleod-Smith. *The faces of love.* Wellington, Harry Tombs, 1964? 114p.
A widower in his late thirties with a young son falls in love with an older woman.

HOWE, A. *Stamper Battery.* Auckland, Blackwood and Janet Paul. 134p.
The author's early life in the goldfields at Thames in the form of a novel.

HUGHES, Ivy. *Halo round the moon.* London, Hale; Christchurch, Whitcombe & Tombs. 187p.
Domestic problems in the Auckland district in the 1860s.

JAY, Simon, pseudonym of Dr Colin James Alexander. *Death of a skin diver.* London, Collins for the Crime Club. 256p, map.
Dr Peter Much, the detective, is a pathologist in Auckland.

JEFFERY, Gretchen Constance Emilie (Weyergang), wrote as Margaret Jeffery. *Mairangi.* Christchurch, Pegasus Press. 194p.
A child comes from England to New Zealand to live with her eccentric great-aunt; the ten-year-old girl, an orphan, recounts her growing up.

JOHNSON, Marguerite Maude, pseudonym Rewa Glenn. *A holiday idyll.* Woodcuts by Elizabeth Johnston (pseudonym?). Christchurch, Pegasus Press. 78p.
Three girls — two of them sisters — who live together have a holiday in Queen Charlotte Sound.

LEE, John. *Shiner Slattery.* Auckland, Collins. 173p. Sequel to *Shining with the Shiner*, 1945.
Continues the humorous adventures of a super-tramp.

MARSH, Ngaio. *Dead water.* London, Collins for the Crime Club. 256p.
A death at a rural spa in England requires the expertise of Superintendent Alleyn.

MESSENGER, Elizabeth. *Growing evil.* London, Hale. 192p.
People arrive in Auckland by yacht and are entangled in mystery and death.

MESSENGER, Elizabeth. *You won't need a coat.* London, Hale. 191p.
Why did a young married woman commit suicide?

MORRIESON, Ronald. *Came a hot Friday.* Sydney, Angus & Robertson. 234p.
Racketeers in a small mill town.

OWEN, Doreen May. *A stranger stands.* London, Hale; Christchurch, Whitcombe & Tombs. 239p. Sequel *Not so the land*, 1965.
The captain of a whaler and his young wife arrive in New Zealand in the 1850s.

PETERS, Charles, wrote as Charles Francis. *Ask a river.* London, Hale; Christchurch, Whitcombe & Tombs. 189p.
The body of a young farmer found in the Waikato River brings Inspector Rope to investigate.

PETERS, Charles. *Johnny Rapana.* Christchurch, Whitcombe & Tombs. 190p.
A poorly-educated Maori youth leaves the pa for an exciting life in Auckland and quickly bored settles for girls, liquor and crime.

PRESTON, Ivy. *Hearts do not break.* London, Hale; Christchurch, Whitcombe & Tombs. 192p.
A romance in which a spinster tries to forget heartaches by training as a nurse.

ROBERTSON, Mrs Rita Clarice. *I dare not mourn.* London, Hale; Christchurch, Whitcombe & Tombs.
Romance with an Auckland setting and a widow who marries an American soldier during World War II.

SANDERSON, Nora. *A partner for Doctor Philip.* London, Mills & Boon. 188p.
Romance with a medical background.

SANDERSON, Nora. *Shadows in the ward.* London, Mills & Boon. 191p.
Includes the personal problems of the staff at a hospital in Canterbury.

SANDERSON, Nora. *The taming of Nurse Conway.* London, Mills & Boon. 189p.
A nurse's dislike of one of the doctors.

SAVA, George, pseudonym. *A surgeon in New Zealand.* London, Faber. 220p.
In a brief visit the doctor does some sight-seeing but does not neglect medicine.

SCOTT, Mary. *A change from mutton.* Auckland, Paul. 186p.
Life in a small town told with some humour.

SCOTT, Mary and Joyce West. *No red herrings.* Auckland, Paul; London, Angus & Robertson. 187p.
Disappearance of a girl after returning to New Zealand from Honolulu.

SUMMERS, Essie. *Bride in flight.* London, Mills & Boon. 192p.
A girl about to be married hears some alarming news.

SUMMERS, Essie. *The smoke and the fire.* London, Mills & Boon. 189p.
A girl arriving in New Zealand faces problems with her fiance's mother.

SUMMERS, Essie. *The time and the place.* London, Mills & Boon. 188p.
A South Island romance with a school background.

SUMMERS, Essie. *Where no roads go.* London, Mills & Boon. 190p.
A woman is left with a part-share of a tourist hostel.

TULLETT, James. *Red Abbott.* London, Hale; Christchurch, Whitcombe. 192p.
Former RAF pilot and his younger brother in an aerial topdressing business.

WILSON, Phillip. *Pacific flight.* London, Hale; Christchurch, Whitcombe & Tombs. 192p.
Activities in Auckland and the Pacific of airmen in World War II. Two of them are in love with a Red Cross girl.

WINDER, Mavis, wrote as Mavis Areta. *Love keeps no score.* London, Wright & Brown. 173p.

WORBOYS, Anne. *Visit to Rata Creek.* London, Hurst & Blackett. 183p.
A woman comes to New Zealand to visit her mother's relations and learns more about their lives that had been worrying her.

1965

ADDISON, Doris. *Bird of time.* London, Hale; Christchurch, Whitcombe & Tombs. 220p.
The people of a prosperous rural community.

ADDISON, Doris. *A greenstone of two colours.* London, Hale; Christchurch, Whitcombe & Tombs. 191p.
A woman teacher in the country becomes interested in problems of the Maoris.

AUDLEY, Ernest. *A new gate for Mattie Dulivich.* London, Hodder & Stoughton. 191p.
A Dalmatian farmer in isolated Coromandel.

BALDWIN, Beatrice Lilian. *The red dust.* London, Hale; Christchurch, Whitcombe & Tombs. 190p.
Science fiction set partly in New Zealand with lethal dust creating havoc.

BEVAN, Gloria, pseudonym Fiona Murray. *Invitation to danger.* London, Hale; Christchurch, Whitcombe & Tombs. 191p.
Mystery around Rotorua.

BILLING, Graham John. *Forbush and the penguins.* Wellington, Reed. 191p.
A lone biologist studies penguins in Antarctica. Filmed in England, 1970.

BOOTH, Patrick. *Dear Chevvy.* Illustrations by Keith S. Clark. Wellington, Reed. 128p.
A humorous account of people associated with a vintage car.

BRATHWAITE, Errol. *The needle's eye.* London, Collins. 323p, maps. Sequel to *The flying fish*, 1964. The last of the trilogy is *The evil day*, 1967.
Includes a court martial where the chief character Major Williams is seen as a ruthless soldier who places expediency before justice.

CARMAN, Dulce. *The youngest one.* London, Wright & Brown. 172p.
A girl goes to Napier to work, but she is something of a mystery.

COUMBE, Eric Edwin. *The cold moon of spring.* London, Collins. 205p.
A New Zealand soldier from Korea on leave in Japan.

CRUMP, Barry. *Scrapwaggon.* Illustrations by Roger Hart. Wellington, Reed. 158p.
Two refuse collectors supply the comedy.

DRYLAND, Gordon Boyce. *An absence of angels.* London, Collins, 191p.
A librarian separated from his wife meets an older woman and becomes one of her lovers.

EDEN, Dorothy. *The marriage chest.* London, Hodder & Stoughton. 191p.
Two English women experience macabre occurrences on the island of Grenada in the early 20th century.

FRAME, Janet. *The adaptable man.* Christchurch, Pegasus Press. 270p.
Family life in England where a dentist is indifferent to his wife's ambitions to make him a fashionable practitioner.

GEE, Maurice. *A special flower.* London, Hutchinson. 192p.
Frank study of domestic tensions with a forty-six-year-old married to a woman twenty years his junior and her affair with a football player.

GRAYLAND, Valerie. *Jest of darkness.* London, Hale; Christchurch, Whitcombe & Tombs. 195p.
Hoani Mata, the Maori detective, helps solve further crime.

HILLIARD, Noel. *Power of joy.* London, Joseph. 324p. A sequel to *Maori girl*, 1960, and the second of four novels.
A study of Paul Bennett growing up, his preference for solitude and life at boarding school.

HOLDEN, Anne Jacqueline (Dare). *Rata, a novel about childhood.* Christchurch, Whitcombe & Tombs. 177p.
A study of an eleven-year-old part-Maori girl who comes to the attention of the Welfare Department.

HOLT, Sheila Betty (Archibald), wrote as Betty Holt and Elizabeth Fagan. *Jennifer Grant, New Zealand nurse.* Auckland, Paul. 126p.
Mother (Holt) and daughter write a career story on the training of nurses.

KOCH, Claude F. *A casual company.* New York, Chilton Books. 218p.
United States servicemen in Auckland during World War II.

McKENNY, Kenneth. *The hide-away man.* London, Barrie & Rockliff. 238p.
Ben Cooke prefers rural Queensland and his girl to his wife in Sydney.

MESSENGER, Elizabeth. *The tail of the Dozing Cat.* London, Hale. 191p.
A girl awaits at a motel her fiance, a doctor delayed in Antarctica.

MESSENGER, Elizabeth. *Uncertain quest.* London, Hale. 191p.
Mystery and romance in Fiordland.

OLLIVIER, Mrs Sally T. *Petticoat farm.* London, Collins. 237p.
Five girls on a farm in the 1920s.

OWEN, Doreen. *Not so the land.* London, Hale; Christchurch, Whitcombe & Tombs. 224p.
Sequel to *A stranger stands,* 1964.
The story of Emmeline Carstairs at Port Underwood and elsewhere in the 1830s and 1840s and the changes in the growing colony.

PRESTON, Ivy. *The blue remembered hills.* London, Hale; Christchurch, Whitcombe & Tombs. 191p.
Romance in a South Canterbury sheep farming area.

ROBERTSON, Rita. *The crooked and the narrow.* London, Hale; Christchurch, Whitcombe & Tombs. 192p.
Romance in the Hawke's Bay district.

RUHEN, Olaf. *The broken wing.* Auckland, Minerva. 224p.
Bombing raids over Germany in World War II.

S.S. *His own enemy; the story of an alcoholic.* Auckland, Blackwood & Janet Paul. 200p.
The study in the form of a novel of a soldier returning from World War II who resumes farming and has a severe affliction. Some libraries classify it as non-fiction.

SANDERSON, Nora. *The case for Nurse Sheridan.* London, Mills & Boon. 192p.
A staff nurse experiences the problems of seeking promotion.

SARGESON, Frank. *Memoirs of a peon.* London, MacGibbon & Kee. 288p.
The amorous life of a 20th century Casanova in Auckland where the great lover is training for teaching.

SCOTT, Mary. *Freddie.* Hamilton, Paul. 178p.
Sequel to *Families are fun,* 1956, and *No sad songs,* 1960.
Freddie, now a qualified nurse, postpones her wedding when her father is sick.

SCOTT, Mary and Joyce West. *Who put it there?* Auckland, Blackwood & Janet Paul; London, Angus & Robertson. 174p.
A body is discovered in the boot of a woman's car.

SHADBOLT, Maurice Francis Richard. *Among the cinders.* Christchurch, Whitcombe & Tombs. 301p.
A humorous account of a sixteen-year-old schoolboy in the process of attaining manhood and his irascible grandfather.

TARRANT, Noeline. *Dead on noon.* London, Hale; Christchurch, Whitcombe & Tombs. 189p.
A reporter and his girl in Rotorua get more than a quiet weekend.

TULLETT, James. *White pine.* London, Hale; Christchurch, Whitcombe & Tombs. 191p.
The story is connected with the forestry industry and the threat of witchcraft hovers over the area.

WATSON, Jean. *Stand in the rain.* Christchurch, Pegasus Press. 150p.
A girl finds congenial a restless life with a man who prefers hunting and fishing to domesticity.

WILSON, Phillip. *The outcasts.* London, Hale; Christchurch, Whitcombe & Tombs. 192p. Sequel *New Zealand Jack,* 1973.
Maori-white problems confront a former soldier and football player and the daughter of a wealthy family.

WINDER, Mavis. *River in the valley.* London, Hale; Christchurch, Whitcombe & Tombs. 192p.
A romance about a New Zealander who is injured in a plane crash and unknown to his family returns home.

WINDER, Mavis. *Scent of the woods.* London, Hale; Christchurch, Whitcombe & Tombs. 189p.
A romance set in the pioneering days.

WORBOYS, Anne. *The valley of yesterday.* London, Hurst & Blackett. 183p.
A romance on a sheep farm in Northland.

1966

ASHTON-WARNER, Sylvia. *Greenstone.* New York, Simon & Schuster. 217p.
There is much Maori lore in this novel of a school teacher who is the grand daughter of a Maori princess.

BALLANTYNE, David. *A friend of the family.* London, Hale; Christchurch, Whitcombe & Tombs. 224p.
Modern city life confusing to a bachelor.

BATES, Peter. *The red mountain.* London, Hale; Christchurch, Whitcombe & Tombs. 176p.
Three New Zealand prisoners-of-war escaping to Switzerland after the collapse of Italy in World War II.

BENNETT, Francis Oswald. *The tenth home.* Auckland, Paul. 178p.
Life in a home for old ladies. The author is a doctor.

BOOTH, Patrick. *Sprint from the bell.* London, Collins. 254p.
After training for the priesthood the protagonist becomes a champion athlete.

EDEN, Dorothy. *Never call it loving.* London, Hodder & Stoughton. 319p.
The love affair between the Irish politician Charles Stewart Parnell and Mrs Kitty O'Shea.

EWEN, J. M. *Far from the sun.* London, Hale; Christchurch, Whitcombe & Tombs. 192p.
Set in a coal-mining area of the South Island where conflicts are frequent.

HAMMOND, Theodore Peter. *This man's father had my father's farm.* Illustrations by Jack Morgan. Wellington, Reed. 149p.
A humorous tale of farm life in Northland with a well-meaning father.

HOUGHTON, Philip. *The shadow of the land.* London, Hodder & Stoughton. 224p.
Dr Houghton writes about a man living in a strange isolated community by the sea.

HUGHES, Ivy. *A falcon rising.* London, Hale. 189p.
A girl flees from England in the 1840s and is in Kororareka at the time of Hone Heke.

HUNTER, Harriet. *Inclination to murder.* London, Hale. 190p.
'These things might happen in the London Underground or the New York Subway, but here in New Zealand — never!'

McCLENAGHAN, John Nathaniel. *Moving target.* Wellington, Reed. 192p.
A former deer culler rebels against army discipline during World War II and deserts to the bush, eluding capture over a long period.

MARSH, Ngaio. *Killer Dolphin.* Boston, Little Brown. 304p. Presumably the story published by Collins in 1967 under the title *Death at the Dolphin.* Centred on a theatre and a playwright who wants to own it.

MASON, Henrietta. *High Acres.* London, Hale; Christchurch, Whitcombe & Tombs. 206p. Sequel to *Our hills cry woe!* 1963, and the last of the trilogy.
A man's dilemma; a life on the family sheep farm or to become a scientist?

NEATE, Frank Anthony. *The hour-glass girl.* Auckland, Paul. 187p.
Problems arise when a forty-two-year-old business man takes a teenage girl home after a party.

ST. BRUNO, Francis. *Riggermortis.* London, Hale. 188p.
The story of a tough professional boxer in Australia.

SCOTT, Mary. *What does it matter?* London, Hurst & Blackett. 183p.
A girl involved in other people's problems.

SCOTT, Nicholas D. *The lancet and the land.* London, Heinemann. 279p.
A newly-qualified doctor from Scotland comes to New Zealand in the 1850s.

STAPLES, Marjory Charlotte (Jefcoate), wrote as Rosaline Redwood. *Forgotten heritage.* London, Hale; Christchurch, Whitcombe & Tombs. 191p.
An American journalist visiting New Zealand discovers something about his ancestors.

STEPHENSON, Ralph. *Down among the dead men.* London, John Gifford. 158p.
A murder is planned with the prospect of making millions.

THOMPSON, Nola Dilyse (Payne). *The share milkers; a novel of the Waikato.* Auckland, Paul. 185p.
A woman describes her life on several farms.

TULLETT, James. *Hunting black.* London, Hale; Christchurch, Whitcombe & Tombs. 192p.
Two Americans come to New Zealand for a deer-stalking holiday, with an account of search-and-rescue operations.

WORBOYS, Anne. *Return to bellbird country.* London, Hurst and Blackett. 186p.
A girl returns from England to Rotorua to seek her father.

WYLIE, Cicely. *The language of love.* London, Hale; Christchurch, Whitcombe & Tombs. 176p.
A man from Austria complicates romance for a girl on a farm.

1967

ADDISON, Doris. *Jane.* London, Hale. 192p.
When Jane is killed in a car crash not everyone is certain it is an accident.

ADDISON, Doris. *Morning tide*. London, Hale. 191p.
A new teacher at a sole-charge school in love with a Maori girl.

ANDREWS, Philip. *Terese*. Auckland, Paul. 101p.
The non-academic life of students at the University of Auckland.

BRATHWAITE, Errol. *The evil day*. London, Collins. 382p. Sequel to *The needle's eye*, 1965.
The concluding volume of the trilogy on the Maori-Pakeha wars of the 19th century, involving Major Williams and the Hauhaus in Taranaki.

BURKE, David. *Monday at McMurdo*. Wellington, Reed. 247p, glossary.
There is apprehension in Antarctica when visitors include a woman.

CARMAN, Dulce. *The necklace of El-Hoya*. London, Wright & Brown. 174p.
Mystery and the subconscious, set in New Zealand.

COWLEY, Cassia Joy (Summers). *Nest in a falling tree*. London, Secker & Warburg. 336p.
A spinster in her forties looking after a sick mother has an infatuation for a teenage boy. Filmed in USA, 1971, under the title 'The Night Digger'.

CRUMP, Barry. *The odd spot of bother*. Illustrations by John Crawley. Wellington, Reed. 159p.
A humorous tale of Windy, a strange fellow who wins a substantial lottery.

EDEN, Dorothy. *Winterwood*. London, Hodder & Stoughton. 251p.
Italy and a stately house in England with a mystery.

FRAME, Janet. *A state of siege*. London, W. H. Allen. 246p.
After retirement and the death of her mother an art teacher moves from her home town to begin a new life. Filmed in New Zealand 1978.

GILBERT, Manu, pseudonym? *Lineman's ticket*. Auckland, Paul. 169p.
A humorous story of a gang working on electric power lines in a rural district.

GROVER, Raymond Frank. *Another man's role*. Auckland, Paul. 134p.
A bright headstrong fellow in conflict with the law, told by his friend, a clergyman's son.

HARVEY, Norman Bruce. *One magpie for sorrow*. London, Hale; Christchurch, Whitcombe & Tombs. 190p.
Chinese forces invade New Zealand.

HOLDEN, Anne. *The empty hills*. London, Hale; Christchurch, Whitcombe & Tombs. 220p.
A family in a small town with the young people striving for a better life.

JOSEPH, Michael. *The hole in the zero*. Auckland, Paul. 191p.
The warder of station Gamma Seventeen plays a major role in a science fiction tale of considerable scope.

JOURNET, Terence Harry. *The death wishers*. London, Hale. 192p.
A mystery begins at a chair lift on Mt Ruapehu.

LAMBE, Zoe Violetta (Lane). *Murder by court martial*. London, Hale; Christchurch, Whitcombe & Tombs. 191p.
New Zealand in the 1840s with an army officer in love with the daughter of a rebel chief.

McLEOD, Mrs Catherine Styles. *Dorinda*. Christchurch, Pegasus Press. 140p.
Dorinda, a widow, does not lack admirers in this novel narrated by her daughter.

OWEN, Maurice. *White mantle*. London, Hale; Christchurch, Whitcombe & Tombs. 192p.
A United States scientist in Antarctica observes changes that could envelop the world; science fiction.

POTHAN, Kap. *A time to die*. Brisbane, Jacaranda Press. 192p.
Australia is invaded by an Asian nation.

SARGESON, Frank. *The hangover*. London, MacGibbon & Kee. 160p.
The problems of an emotionally unsettled young man with a puritan background living with his mother and studying at a university.

SCOTT, Mary. *Yes, darling*. London, Hurst & Blackett. 183p.
A woman leaves the city to live in the country and do some writing.

SHADBOLT, Maurice. *The presence of music; three novellas*. London, Cassell. 213p.
The title story, pages 41-171, is about people who were at school together in a small town; the main character is a journalist who has relationships with several women. The voyagers, pages 1-40, is a study of two men from different backgrounds and a girl. Figures in light, pages 173-213, describes a brother-sister relationship.

STAPLES, Marjory. *Isle of the golden pearls*. London, Hale. 191p.
After an education in New Zealand a young part-Rarotongan woman returns to the isolated Pacific island where she was born.

WINDER, Mavis. *The glitter and the gold*. London, Hale; Christchurch, Whitcombe & Tombs. 187p.
A woman with a domineering attitude towards some of her relatives.

1968

BALLANTYNE, David. *Sydney Bridge upside down.* London, Hale; Christchurch, Whitcombe & Tombs. 223p.
Strange events occur one summer when a pretty girl comes to stay with relatives at an isolated beach community.

BATES, Peter. *Man out of mind.* London, Hale; Christchurch, Whitcombe & Tombs. 191p.
The problems of a young engineer when he assumes control of a road construction company.

BENNETT, Margot. *The furious masters.* London, Eyre & Spottiswoode. 239p.
Set in Yorkshire where an apparent spacecraft creates interest, problems and hysteria.

BRODIE, Gordon. *The lady had a tiger.* London, Hale. 192p.
Crime thriller set in Auckland.

BRODIE, Gordon. *The poison of poppies.* London, Hale. 189p.
Instead of enjoying a holiday a detective's friend gives the police assistance in apprehending criminals.

FRAME, Janet. *The Rainbirds.* London, W. H. Allen. Published in New York by Braziller under the title *Yellow flowers in the antipodean room,* 1969. 206p.
A thirty-year-old English immigrant, ostensibly killed in an accident, is only in a coma; his new situation creates difficulties in readjusting to those around him.

HOLDEN, Anne. *Death after school.* London, Hale; Christchurch, Whitcombe & Tombs. 188p.
Mystery at a secondary modern school in London where a New Zealand woman is teaching.

HUGHES, Ivy. *The Barrier.* London, Hale; Christchurch, Whitcombe & Tombs. 192p.
Two women on Great Barrier Island in love with the same man; sensational events in 1886.

JAY, Simon. *Sleepers can kill.* London, Collins. 256p.
Espionage in New Zealand.

JOHNSON, Marguerite Maud, pseudonym Rewa Glenn. *The turn of the tide.* Woodcuts by Elizabeth Johnston. Christchurch, Pegasus Press. 101p, map.
A romance about a returned soldier-teacher in Queen Charlotte Sound.

JOURNET, Terence. *The god killers.* London, Hale. 190p.
Who had travelled on the night ferry from Wellington to Lyttleton on Robbie Lang's ticket?

McGREGOR, Miriam Florence. *The glowing dark.* London, Hale. 188p.
Love, mystery and death around Waitomo where a girl takes a job and learns that her predecessor had been killed.

MARSH, Ngaio. *Clutch of constables.* London, Collins for the Crime Club. 253p.
Alleyn investigates murders on a boat on English canals in 'Constable' country.

MOORE, Mary. *Where kowhai blooms.* London, Mills & Boon. 160p.
When a girl arrives at Lake Wahine sheep station she is told that women are not allowed there.

MUTCH, Karin. *Wildcat.* London, Mills & Boon. 190p.
A rebellious sixteen-year-old Auckland girl is a problem to her guardian.

PRESTON, Ivy. *Red roses for a nurse.* London, Hale; Christchurch, Whitcombe & Tombs. 191p.
A girl goes to a farm to look after her crippled uncle.

SANDERSON, Nora. *No bells were ringing.* London, Mills & Boon. 192p.
A girl returns to New Zealand intending to marry her childhood sweetheart, but there is another man.

SANDERSON, Nora. *No welcome for Nurse Jane.* London, Mills & Boon. 188p.
A nurse is informed that a particular hospital might prove too difficult for her.

SCOTT, Mary. *Turkey at twelve.* London, Hurst & Blackett. 183p.
An attractive woman from England discovers in the backblocks that she is not popular with other women.

SLATTER, Gordon. *The pagan game.* London, Hale; Christchurch, Whitcombe & Tombs. 239p.
A week in the lives of people associated with rugby football at a secondary school.

STAPLES, Marjory. *Stranger from Shanghai.* London, Hale. 191p.
Intrigue on a cargo vessel carrying a few passengers including New Zealanders around South-East Asia.

SUMMERS, Essie. *Rosalind comes home.* London, Mills & Boon. 191p.
A girl and her stepbrother.

WINDER, Mavis. *The fanned flame.* London, Hale; Christchurch, Whitcombe & Tombs. 189p.
A girl comes to New Zealand for her brother's wedding and is surprised to learn that it is cancelled.

ANDREWS, Isobel Smith (Young). *Return to Marara.* London, Hale; Christchurch, Whitcombe & Tombs. 256p, glossary.
A woman returning to a town after fourteen years for its centennial observes many changes.

BEVAN, Gloria. *The distant trap.* London, Mills & Boon. 190p.
A girl arrives in New Zealand to meet her fiance but he is missing from his farm.

BEVAN, Gloria. *The hills of Maketu.* London, Mills & Boon. 188p.
A girl from the city takes on a job at a sheep station.

BILLING, Graham. *The Alpha trip.* Christchurch, Whitcombe & Tombs. 240p.
Alpha is a secret United States base in New Zealand and in addition to providing an interesting story of espionage, includes science, current politics and nuclear war.

BLISS, Alice. *Spring in the bishop's palace; a novella.* Atlanta, USA, Bozart Press. 84p.
An English girl has a succession of jobs during a brief stay in New Zealand. By an American author who was briefly in New Zealand in the 1950s.

BURFIELD, Eva. *Give them swing bands.* London, Hale; Christchurch, Whitcombe & Tombs. 190p.
Maori-European neighbours are friendly and then there is an accusation of rape.

DORMAN, Thomas Edwin. *The days after.* New York, Vantage Press. 248p.
World War III and after in Africa in the 1970s.

DUCKWORTH, Marilyn. *Over the fence is out.* London, Hutchinson. 191p.
An unfaithful boorish husband, his wife and mistress, set in London and New Zealand.

GRAHAM, Timothy M. A. *The paper man.* Adelaide, Rigby. 308p.
The newspaper world in Melbourne as seen by a New Zealand reporter.

HILLIARD, Noel. *A night at Green River.* London, Hale; Christchurch, Whitcombe & Tombs. 160p.
Maori and pakeha relationships and values in a farming district.

JACKSON, Laurence. *Mana.* London, Stanmore Press. 206p, glossary.
Maori-pakeha land problems in the 19th century.

KEINZLEY, Frances. *A time to prey.* London, W. H. Allen. 189p.
A mystery story involving the blackmail of several Aucklanders.

McCLENAGHAN, Jack. *The ice admiral.* Christchurch, Whitcombe & Tombs. 238p.
United States rescue operations in Antarctica and the lives of some personnel in Christchurch.

McGREGOR, Miriam. *The drifting mist.* London, Hale. 191p.
A mystery romance of a girl intereted in painting, on the trail of a perplexing uncle.

McGREGOR, Miriam. *The whispering echo.* London, Hale. 192p.
Taken to England when a baby, a young woman returns to New Zealand to a homestead surrounded by mystery.

MASON, Francis van Wyck. *Harpoon in Eden.* New York, Doubleday. 430p.
Sperm whaling in the 1830s set in the United States and New Zealand, by an American author.

MOORE, Mary. *Rata flowers are red.* London, Mills & Boon. 188p.
An engaged girl has problems with her prospective mother-in-law.

MUTCH, Karin. *Cindy tread lightly.* London, Mills & Boon. 189p.
Cindy Taylor is apprehensive about a man who is determined in his advances towards her.

NOONAN, Michael. *The pink beach.* London, Hale. 192p.
Humorous story set in Australia of a woman and her small son who becomes a jockey.

PHIPPS, Grace. *No wife for a parson.* London, Hale. 189p.
A girl tramper after losing her money takes a job at a beach store.

PRESTON, Ivy. *April in Westland.* London, Hale; Christchurch, Whitcombe & Tombs. 189p.
A girl finds the West Coast not as dull a place as she had anticipated.

PRESTON, Ivy. *Ticket of destiny.* London, Hale; Christchurch, Whitcombe & Tombs. 192p.
A romance about two girls who get a prize in a lottery and go to Australia for a holiday.

PRIOR, Anne. *Mirror image.* London. Chatto & Windus. 215p. Sequel to *The sky cage.*
A rebellion is planned in a country suppressed by an army of occupation.

QUENTIN, Dorothy. *Goldenhaze.* London, Mills & Boon. 190p.
A bereavement prompts an English girl to fly to New Zealand.

ROOKE, Daphne Marie. *Boy on the mountain.* London, Gollancz. 192p.
Secondary school boys and girls involved in mountain climbing and tragedies in the South Island.

RUHEN, Olaf. *Scan the dark coast.* London, Hodder & Stoughton. 223p.
A New Zealand coast watcher in the Solomon Islands fighting the Japanese in World War II.

SANDERSON, Nora. *Stranger to the truth.* London, Mills & Boon. 192p.
On her first visit to New Zealand a woman who can fly a plane masquerades as someone else.

SARGESON, Frank. *Joy of the worm.* London, MacGibbon & Kee. 159p.
The work, often in the form of letters, describes the relationship between a pedantic Methodist minister and his son, a county clerk who becomes a school teacher.

SCOTT, Mary. *Strictly speaking.* London, Hurst & Blackett; Auckland, Hutchinson. 183p.
Two women set up a tea room in the country.

SHADBOLT, Maurice. *This summer's dolphin.* London, Cassell. 166p.
Motutangi, an offshore island and a popular holiday resort, comes alive when a friendly dolphin arouses national interest and affects the lives of a number of people.

SNELLER, Jean. *Heart of gold.* London, Hale. 192p.
A teacher comes to a sole charge rural school and is the first woman to hold the position.

SUMMERS, Essie. *The kindled fire.* London, Mills & Boon. 188p.
A teenage girl and an older man part company so she can be certain she will later want to settle down.

SUMMERS, Essie. *Revolt — and Virginia.* London, Mills & Boon. 191p.
A young woman deserts the city to escape two suitors and meets a third.

SWIFT, Rachelle, pseudonym of Jean Lumsden. *The house at Green Bay.* London, Hale. 192p.
Mystery and romance. New Zealand is not quite the paradise a visitor imagined.

WINDER, Mavis. *The lamp in the window* by Mavis Areta Wynder. London, Oliphants. 126p.
The daughter of a wealthy man experiences difficulties when she becomes a minister's wife.

1970

ASHTON-WARNER, Sylvia. *Three.* New York, Knopf. 241p.
A study in the relationships of a New Zealand woman, her son and his French wife, set in London.

BATES, Peter. *Old men are fools.* London, Hale; Christchurch, Whitcombe & Tombs. 189p.
Romance, illicit drugs, police and politics.

BEVAN, Gloria. *Beyond the ranges.* London, Mills & Boon. 189p.
Lesley Monteith inherits property in New Zealand and deserts her London bedsitter for a new country.

BRENT, Marama. *Sigh for Selina.* London, Hale. 191p.
Unhappy in love a twenty-two-year-old girl leaves the city to work with a friend, the wife of a vicar.

BURFIELD, Eva. *To the garden alone.* London, Hale; Christchurch, Whitcombe & Tombs. 350p.
Following the death of her husband a woman boards a nurse and a Maori working man.

COWLEY, Joy. *Man of straw.* London, Secker & Warburg. 227p.
Story of a family which includes an unfaithful husband and two daughters, one a teacher, the other a thirteen-year-old tomboy.

CRUMP, Barry. *A good keen girl.* Illustrations by Tony Stones. Wellington, Reed. 155p.
Humorous tale of a man acquiring a wife.

DAVIN, Daniel. *Not here, not now.* London, Hale; Christchurch, Whitcombe & Tombs. 350p.
Dunedin in the depression years of the 1930s when Martin Cody is a university student who subsequently becomes a Rhodes Scholar.

EDEN, Dorothy. *Waiting for Willa.* London, Hodder & Stoughton. 185p.
A suspense novel set in Sweden where a woman has gone to locate a former school friend.

FRAME, Janet. *Intensive care; a novel.* New York, Braziller. 342p.
The impact of World War I on a soldier. A study of loneliness and death, and the chronicle of a family.

GIBSON, Colin. *The love-keeper.* London, Chatto & Windus. 203p.
A young English actress visits Rome where she experiences a varied sex life.

HENAGHAN, Rosalie. *The sophisticated urchin.* London, Mills & Boon. 190p.
A romance about a couple who were childhood friends.

HUGHES, Ivy. *The house at Stormy Waters.* London, Hale; Christchurch, Whitcombe & Tombs. 188p.
A romance with a girl helping a part-Maori boy in trouble; and an inheritance.

JOSEPH, George. *Take any city.* London, Hale; Christchurch, Whitcombe & Tombs. 159p.
A famous English author abandons his problems and comes to New Zealand.

KEINZLEY, Frances. *Illusion.* London, W. H. Allen. 286p.
Death comes to a young woman following an affair and an abortion, and retribution is planned.

LEE, John. *Mussolini's millions.* London, Harold Baker. 207p.
A thriller set in New Zealand where a former prisoner-of-war James Burns discovers war loot in a cave.

McGREGOR, Miriam. *Hasten to danger.* London, Hale. 192p.
A young woman's life is threatened before love overcomes all.

McKENNY, Kenneth. *The orderly.* London, Deutsch. 253p.
A Fijian orderly in a London hospital.

McLEOD, Catherine. *Fortunately there was a haystack.* London, W. H. Allen; Wellington, Reed. 141p.
The story of an Auckland girl at the university who writes a novel, and its effect on her family.

McNEISH, James Henry Peter. *Mackenzie; a novel.* London, Hodder & Stoughton. 384p.
This work is based on the drover and sheep stealer, James Mackenzie, who in the middle of the 19th century was supposed to have discovered the Mackenzie Country.

MARSH, Ngaio. *When in Rome.* London, Collins for the Crime Club. 256p.
A problem within a tour party leads to Alleyn assisting the police in Rome.

MICHAEL, Shona. *The season at Sunrise.* London, Hale; Christchurch, Whitcombe & Tombs. 189p.
Sunrise Bay, usually a dull place, comes alive over the Christmas holidays when a diversity of people pour into it.

MUTCH, Karin. *The story of Jody.* London, Mills & Boon. 191p.
A city girl on probation works on a farm near Palmerston North.

NETHERCOTE, Ron. *The merciless.* Wellington, Reed. 223p.
After Greece is defeated by the Germans in 1941 the local guerillas are joined by Australian soldiers.

PRESTON, Ivy. *A fleeting breath.* London, Hale; Wellington, Whitcombe & Tombs. 191p.
A girl achieves success as a singer but longs for her childhood sweetheart.

SANDERSON, Nora. *A place in the sun.* London, Mills & Boon. 188p.
A romance about a man who wants to farm and a girl who loathes life in the country.

SCOTT, Mary. *Haven't we met before?* London, Hurst & Blackett. 184p.
Set in the backblocks with an unconventional girl who paints.

SUMMERS, Essie. *The bay of the nightingales.* London, Mills & Boon. 188p.
A girl comes to New Zealand to search for her father.

SUMMERS, Essie. *Summer in December.* London, Mills & Boon. 188p.
Romance on a sheep station.

SWIFT, Rachel. *A taunt from the past.* London, Hale; Christchurch, Whitcombe & Tombs. 192p.
Romance and mystery in a Wellington department store.

SWIFT, Rachel. *Vicky.* London, Hale. 157p.
A mystery surrounding a missing girl.

TAYLOR, William. *Episode.* London, Hale; Christchurch, Whitcombe & Tombs. 157p.
A school teacher dismissed for sexual misconduct meets an understanding Maori woman.

TAYLOR, William. *The mask of the clown.* London, Hale; Christchurch, Whitcombe & Tombs. 189p.
Entertainment comes 'to the sticks' with the arrival of an elderly magician and a youthful pop star.

THIAN, Valeria Joan. *O kiss me Kate.* London, Mills & Boon. 187p.
Two sisters and the men in their lives.

TULLETT, James. *Town of fear.* London, Hale; Christchurch, Whitcombe & Tombs. 159p.
While sitting in a plane delayed in landing, lawyer Bernard Jackson reviews his life.

WORBOYS, Anne. *The little millstones.* London, Hurst & Blackett. 183p.
Romance in Poverty Bay.

1971

ANDREWS, Isobel. *Exit with emeralds.* London, Hale; Christchurch, Whitcombe & Tombs. 223p.
Jacquetta Barlow creates a few problems when she comes to Greenhills.

ARMFELT, Nicholas. *Catching up.* London, Faber. 245p.
An immigrant teacher in New Zealand becomes involved with one of his adolescent girl students.

BENNETT, Francis Oswald. *March of the little men.* Wellington, Reed. 254p.
The story of people in a rural township in Canterbury between the two world wars.

BEVAN, Gloria. *It began in Te Rangi*. London, Mills & Boon. 191p.
'No more engagement rings for her — ever.' Then a sheep farmer needs a housekeeper.

BEVAN, Gloria. *Make way for tomorrow*. London, Mills & Boon. 188p.
A girl leaves London for a holiday in North Auckland with her aunt and uncle.

BEVAN, Gloria, pseudonym Fiona Murray. *A nice day for murder*. London, Hale 190p.
A thriller with a New Zealand setting.

BILLING, Graham. *Statues*. London, Hodder & Stoughton. 255p.
A study of people and art with a television personality leaving his job to create a garden of statues.

CLEARY, Frances. *This Mrs Kingi*. Auckland, Collins. 147p. Sequel *A pocketful of years*, 1975.
A Maori grandmother in the Bay of Islands tells humorously of her life.

CRUMP, Barry. *'No reference intended.'* Wellington, Reed. 164p. Illustrations.
A humorous account of the experiences of a journalist including an hilarious description of an assignment in the country.

GIBSON, Colin. *The pepper leaf; an episode*. London, Chatto & Windus. 231p.
A strange tale of four isolated people during a nuclear fallout; a young girl is a dominating character.

GRAYLAND, Valerie, pseudonym Lee Belvedere. *Farewell to a valley*. New York, Bouregy. 151p.
When her brother marries, a twenty-one-year-old girl leaves their farm for a different kind of life.

HOLDEN, Anne. *The witnesses*. London, Macmillan. 191p.
From a flat window a girl sees a person attacked but is reluctant to give the police information.

HOOKER, John. *Jacob's season*. London, Barrie & Jenkins. 188p.
Some odd characters in a bawdy tale.

HUTCHINSON, Ivy. *Forbidden marriage; a factual story of early settlers in Thames and on the coast*. Auckland, printed by Pelorus Press. 172p.
A true story in the form of a novel of a young couple during gold mining days in the 19th century.

JEFFERY, Margaret. *Tree without shade*. London, Hale. 200p.
Life on a Hawke's Bay sheep farm.

LUSON, Pamela. *Julia*. London, Hodder & Stoughton. 223p.
Julia Newcombe, mother of a large family in 19th century England, is the main character in a story based on fact.

McGREGOR, Miriam. *The house at Lake Taupo*. London, Hale. 189p.
Strangers appear at a house on the shore of the lake.

McGREGOR, Miriam. *Sails of destiny* by Helen Pegden, pseudonym. London, Hale. 189p.
A girl is tricked into sailing to New Zealand in the 1840s.

MOORE, Mary. *Along the ribbonwood track*. London, Mills & Boon. 189p.
A woman arrives in New Zealand to take possession of a farm left by her grandfather and encounters opposition.

MULCOCK, Anne. *Landscape with figures*. London, Hale; Christchurch, Whitcombe & Tombs. 239p.
The middle-aged wife of a prosperous Canterbury farmer becomes bored with dull routine so tries painting and takes a lover.

MUTCH, Karin Maureen. *Eve's own Eden*. London, Mills & Boon. 192p.
A romance set on a farm.

MUTCH, Karin. *No saints on this highway*. London, Mills & Boon. 158p.
A nineteen-year-old girl who likes to be free roams the highways with her guitar.

PHIPPS, Grace. *The bridal boutique*. London, Hale. 191p.
One of two girls flatting together in Wellington runs a shop for wedding clothes.

PRESTON, Ivy. *Portrait of Pierre*. London, Hale; Christchurch, Whitcombe & Tombs. 182p.
A mystery develops when a woman goes to Dunedin to inspect a property she has inherited.

SANDERS, James Edward. *The green paradise*. London, Hale; Christchurch, Whitcombe & Tombs. 224p.
The ship Boyd left convicts in Australia before proceeding to New Zealand. Her passengers have some surprising experiences.

SANDERSON, Nora. *Come in from the cold*. London, Mills & Boon. 192p.
A girl at university in Wellington and involved in the protest movement avoids conflict with the law by working on a South Island farm.

SCOTT, Mary. *If I don't, who will?* Auckland, Hutchinson. 182p.
On her grandmother's death, a woman inherits a house and children.

SHADBOLT, Maurice. *An ear of the dragon*. London, Cassell. 282p.
A writer visits the widow of his late poet friend and the relationships of the three are explored; set partly in Italy during World War II and later in New Zealand.

SOPER, Eileen Louise (Service). *The month of the brittle star.* Line drawings by Ione Todd. Dunedin, McIndoe. 93p.
A study of an adolescent girl absorbed in nature.

STEAD, Christian Karlson. *Smith's dream.* Auckland, Longman Paul. 142p.
Smith, a man hunted by the authorities, joins other rebels in the Coromandel area and they are hunted by United States Special Forces. The last few pages were rewritten for the 1973 paperback edition. Filmed in New Zealand under the title Sleeping Dogs, *1977.*

SUMMERS, Essie. *The house in Gregor's brae.* London, Mills & Boon. 191p.
A girl's life is altered by her meeting an author.

SUMMERS, Essie. *Return to Dragonshill.* London, Mills & Boon. 191p.
A widow is offered a future by a former sweetheart.

SWIFT, Rachelle. *Romance for Judith.* London, Hale; Christchurch, Whitcombe & Tombs. 191p.
A girl goes to Queenstown to forget love, but is soon enmeshed again.

TAYLOR, William. *The Plekhov place.* London, Hale. 223p.
What were the facts about the White Russians living in New Zealand?

WILSON, Trevor E. *Knock softly on death's door.* London, Hale; Christchurch, Whitcombe & Tombs. 190p.
Drug ring problems.

WORBOYS, Anne. *Rainbow child.* London, Hurst & Blackett. 183p.
A romance with an Australian setting.

1972

CAMERON, Ian. *The mountains at the bottom of the world.* London, Hodder & Stoughton. 212p.

COWLEY, Joy. *Of men and angels.* London, Hodder & Stoughton; New York, Doubleday. 279p.
Almost entirely in dialogue, the novel is about two women of diverse character and a pregnant girl they befriend.

CRUMP, Barry. *Fred.* Illustrations by Howard Baker. Auckland, Crump Productions. 109p.
Humorous story of life on the West Coast.

DAVIN, Daniel. *Brides of price.* London, Hale; Christchurch, Whitcombe & Tombs. 254p.
A middle-aged Oxford academic writes of the women in his life. The novel includes publishing, World War II, the university and New Zealand.

EDEN, Dorothy. *Speak to me of love.* London, Hodder & Stoughton. 352p.
The life of an ambitious woman in Victorian England.

FERGUSON, Sir Bernard Edward. *Captain John Niven.* Auckland, Collins. 127p.
Biographical novel based on the life of John Bollons who at the age of sixteen was shipwrecked off the New Zealand coast and spent some years living with Maoris. The author was Governor-General of New Zealand 1962-67 and later took the title Lord Ballantrae.

FRAME, Janet. *Daughter Buffalo.* New York, Braziller. 212p.
Set mainly in the United States where an American-Jewish doctor and a New Zealand writer display a considerable interest in death.

GEE, Maurice. *In my father's den.* London, Faber. 175p.
A secondary school teacher is the narrator in this novel in which he is suspected of the murder of one of his students, a seventeen-year-old girl.

GRAYLAND, Valerie, pseudonym Lee Belvedere. *Thunder Beach.* New York, Thomas Bouregy, Avalon Books. 190p.
A coastal town receives a lot of publicity when a millionaire's yacht is wrecked.

GRAYLAND, Valerie, pseudonym Lee Belvedere. *Fringe of heaven.* New York, Thomas Bouregy, Avalon Books. 190p.

KELLY, Maurice. *Mandarin's way.* Auckland, Pagoda Publications. 210p.
A political novel with a former New Zealand lawyer involved in the struggle for Indo-China.

McKENNY, Kenneth. *The terminator.* London, Talmy Franklin. 256p.
A school teacher in England becomes a back street abortionist with some alarming results for his patients and himself.

MARSH, Ngaio. *Tied up in tinsel.* London, Collins. 256p.
Some unusual servants are employed at an English manor at Christmas where among the guests is Alleyn's wife.

NEWTON, Peter. *Sheep thief.* London, Hale. 189p.
A man is given the task of investigating sheep stealing at two high country sheep stations.

PENBERTHY, Brent. *The shallow end.* London, Hale; Christchurch, Whitcombe & Tombs. 189p.
The making of a documentary film on a Maori-pakeha marriage.

PHIPPS, Grace. *And be my love.* London, Hale. 189p.
A kindergarten teacher discovers love.

RITCHIE, Kevin W. *From the south.* Invercargill, Times Printing Service. 140p, map.
An adolescent pakeha boy first captured then adopted by Maoris in the 19th century.

SANDERS, James. *The shores of wrath.* London, Hale. 208p.
In 1801 Kate Hagerty is one of many convicts on a ship to Australia and later goes to New Zealand.

SARGESON, Frank. *Man of England now* with *I for one...* and *A game of hide and seek.* Christchurch, Caxton Press. 233p.
Man of England now, pages 11-74. After World War I a Lancashire man and his wife migrate to New Zealand and suffer a number of hardships. I for one, pages 77-149; see 1952. A game of hide and seek, pages 151-233. A man living in Auckand writes of meetings with his father and other people he knows, including a Samoan.

SCOTT, Mary. *Shepherd's pie.* London, Hurst & Blackett. 183p.
A girl in the country falls in love with a young doctor.

SHADBOLT, Maurice. *Strangers and journeys.* London, Hodder & Stoughton. 636p.
The lives of two men and their families between World War I and the 1960s; one man a returned serviceman and a farmer, the other a conscientious objector and trade unionist.

SWIFT, Rachelle. *I, Louise.* London, Hale. 190p.
A young widow returns to England from Canada to begin life afresh.

TAYLOR, William. *The persimmon tree.* London, Hale; Christchurch, Whitcombe & Tombs. 207p.
The elder son tells the wretched story of his family living on a farm, the father a former All Black.

TAYLOR, William. *Pieces in a jigsaw.* London, Hale. 223p.
A woman teacher, and students including a Maori girl, at a secondary school in a small town.

WILSON, Trevor. *Fugitive from fear.* London, Hale; Christchurch, Whitcombe & Tombs. 191p.
'He was willing to die for her but they were slow in giving him the opportunity to test his new resolve.' A thriller concerning a security agent.

WORDSWORTH, Jane. *Four women.* London, Hale; Christchurch, Whitcombe & Tombs. 189p.
Maori and pakeha cultures and relationships seen through the lives of two Maori women and two white women.

1973

ALLEY, Rewi. *Prisoners Shanghai, 1936.* Christchurch, Caxton Press. 58p.
Written during Chiang Kai-shek's anti-Communist rebellion and based on true stories.

BATES, Peter. *A kind of treason.* London, Hale. 190p.
A former war hero is connected with some dubious activities.

BEVAN, Gloria. *Fame in Fiji.* London, Mills & Boon. 189p.
A girl goes to Fiji to assist her brother in running a guest house.

BILLING, Graham. *The slipway.* New York, Viking Press. 216p.
The head of a declining coastal shipping firm has a problem with alcohol.

CONSTABLE, Lawrence. *The house without windows.* London, Milton House Books, Dolphin Publishing Company. 318p.
Adventures in Morocco.

DENMAN, Peter. *The man who guided missiles.* London, Hale; Christchurch, Whitcombe & Tombs. 188p.
A scientist is kidnapped from a New Zealand advanced missile guidance base. Thriller.

DRYLAND, Gordon. *Balloons.* London, Hale; Christchurch, Whitcombe & Tombs. 224p.
About a man with an athletic body who is a sculptor's model and the women attracted to him.

DRYLAND, Gordon. *A multiple texture.* London, Hale; Christchurch, Whitcombe & Tombs. 192p.
A forty-seven-year-old historian and biographer returns to her homeland New Zealand with her secretary, David Stanhope.

FERNANDEZ, Natalie. *Tussock fever.* Auckland, Boughtwood Printing House. 213p.
Life on a sheep station in Hawke's Bay and a shooting incident.

GANT, Phyllis. *Islands.* London, Hodder & Stoughton. 288p.
An Australian childhood during the 1930s; the secret islands of childhood to be protected from the curious. The author was born in Australia.

GLENDAY, Alice. *Follow, follow.* Auckland, Collins and Auckland City Council. 231p.
After the death of her husband a young woman joins her family at the beach. The novel won the Auckland Centennial Fiction Competition, 1971.

GRAYLAND, Valerie, pseudonym Lee Belvedere.
The smiling house. New York, Avalon Books. 189p.
A romance of a woman who, following the death of her much older husband, becomes interested in his son by a former marriage.

HOARE, Hugh Alan. *Now and forever.* London, Hale. 190p.
A thriller in which a journalist is confronted with some sticky situations.

HOLDEN, Anne. *The girl on the beach.* London, Macmillan. 189p. Also published in New York by Delacorte Press.
A family is curious about a girl when they give her a lift from the beach.

IHIMAERA, Witi Tame. *Tangi.* Auckland, Heinemann. 204p.
Narrated by a young Maori the novel tells of the death of his father; it is concerned with family unity and values of the rural Maori. The first novel by a Maori writer; the work gained first prize as James Wattie Book of the Year 1974.

JEFFERY, Margaret. *Cabin at your gate.* Wellington, Reed. 190p.
A widow and the men in her life.

JOURNET, Terence. *A troup of star-crossed killers.* London, Hale. 188p.
Fiji provides the venue for a thriller.

MANNING, Arthur. *The Prime Minister.* London, Hale; Christchurch, Whitcombe & Tombs. 207p.
Private and public life in the rise of an ambitious man to the top post in New Zealand politics.

MASON, Colin. *Hostage.* London, Macmillan. 221p.
World War Three with its beginnings in Egypt.

MOORE, Mary. *Matai Valley magic.* London, Mills & Boon. 190p.
A young woman hitchhiking is injured in an accident and convalesces at the home of the man in whose car she was travelling.

MUTCH, Karin. *Stepping stones with a rebel.* London, Mills & Boon. 191p.
A university girl becomes interested in a tough, long-haired guy.

NOONAN, Michael. *The sun is God.* London, Barrie & Jenkins. 217p.
Fictional biography of the English painter J. M. W. Turner, 1775-1851.

PEEL, Colin Dudley. *Adapted to stress.* London, Hale. 191p.
Espionage involving Communists.

PEEL, Colin. *Bitter autumn.* London, Hale. 183p.
On the trail of illegally-mined gold.

PEEL, Colin. *One sword less.* London, Hale. 188p.
An engineer and the nuclear power struggle.

PHIPPS, Grace. *The doctor's three daughters.* London, Hale. 191p.
The youngest daughter has a boyfriend but is attracted to her father's partner.

PRESTON, Ivy. *Release the past.* London, Hale; Christchurch, Whitcombe & Tombs. 184p.
After the death of her husband, a woman goes to Canada.

SANDERS, James. *High hills of gold.* London, Hale. 191p.
Gold rush days in the Coromandel in the 1860s with some Australians seeking their fortunes.

SANDERS, James. *Kindred of the winds.* London, Hale. 191p.
An American whaler on its way to New Zealand in the 1830s with the captain's wife on board, pregnant to the second mate.

SCOTT, Mary. *First things first.* London, Hurst & Blackett. 191p.
A librarian and a vet.

SUMMERS, Essie. *The forbidden valley.* London, Mills & Boon. 189p.
A woman arrives in New Zealand to take up a position as a nanny, with an ulterior motive.

SWIFT, Rachelle. *Caroline.* London, Hale. 158p.
A bereaved husband who had married in Paris tries to locate his late wife's family in England.

WENDT, Albert. *Sons for the return home.* Auckland, Longman Paul. 218p, glossary.
A young Samoan has an affair while at university with a local girl who later has an abortion; clash of cultures. The first indigenous novel from the South-West Pacific. Filmed in NZ 1979.

WILSON, Phillip. *New Zealand Jack.* London, Hale. 192p. Sequel to *The outcasts,* 1965.
New Zealand past and present, Maori and pakeha.

WILSON, Trevor. *The parasites.* London, Hale. 176p.
Rangi Maniapoto, an ex-boxer, in love with a pakeha girl, and some events that attract the police.

WINDER, Mavis. *Folly is joy.* London, Hale; Christchurch, Whitcombe & Tombs. 193p.
A girl is apprehended with drugs.

WORBOYS, Anne. *Venetian inheritance.* London, Hurst & Blackett. 191p.
After an unhappy romance an English girl goes to Italy where her grandmother is a contessa.

1974

ADSETT, Delphin Rose. *Leave me in the park.* London, Hale; Christchurch, Whitcombe & Tombs. 191p.
The study of a disturbed young man living in a city boarding house.

BERG, Rilla, pseudonym of Thelma France. *The glitter not the gold.* London, Mills & Boon. 191p.
A nurse who wins a medal in her first year of training has a crush on a doctor.

BEVAN, Gloria. *Connelly's Castle.* London, Mills & Boon. 189p.
A woman goes to New Zealand to see a property she has inherited.

BEVAN, Gloria. *High country wife.* London, Mills & Boon. 187p.
A girl working in the nursery on a ship falls in love with the guardian of one of her charges.

COLLEY, I. B. *Death in the dimness.* London, Hale. 192p.
A murder investigation at a guest house.

DAVIS, George Harold. *The scapegoat.* Hamilton, M. H. Blake. 197p.
The career of a civil servant in the post office revealing anxieties associated with all state services.

DYSON, John. *The prime minister's boat is missing.* London, Angus & Robertson. 255p.
Was the prime minister hijacked during an offshore yachting race in the English Channel?

EDEN, Dorothy. *The millionaire's daughter.* London, Hodder & Stoughton. 285p.
An American girl marries into the English aristocracy and faces difficulties.

HELLIWELL, Arthur. *My dangerous love.* London, Hale. 181p.
A young woman returns to England after living in New Zealand.

HILLIARD, Noel. *Maori woman.* London, Hale; Christchurch, Whitcombe & Tombs. 317p. Sequel to *Maori Girl*, 1960, and *Power of joy*, 1965. Followed by *The Glory and the Dream*, 1978.
Continues the story of Netta Samuel.

IHIMAERA, Witi. *Whanau.* Auckland, Heinemann. 173p.
'Whanau' is the extended Maori family. The novel studies Maoris today and the strain to hold fast to traditional values within the framework and temptations of European society.

JOURNET, Terence Henry. *Victim.* London, Hale. 182p.
A thriller with a funeral that recalls earlier events.

LOCKLEY, Ronald Mathias. *Seal woman.* Illustrations by Robert Gillmor. London, R. Collings. 154p.
A naturalist discovers a seal girl and love.

MACKERSEY, Ian. *Long night's journey.* London, Hale. 192p.
A thriller about a hijacker on the Wellington-Auckland train.

MARSH, Ngaio. *Black as he's painted.* London, Collins for the Crime Club. 254p.
When the African President of Ng'ombwana visits London, Roderick Alleyn is occupied with security arrangements.

MAUGHAN, C. William. *Good and faithful servant.* Palmerston North? Waiata and Imperial Publishing Company. 150 copies printed. Published in 1975 by Cape Catley, with added illustrations. 211p.
A satire on the public service and politics in Wellington.

MOORE, Mary. *Manuka fire.* London, Mills & Boon. 186p.
A young teacher moves to a new environment to forget her problems but there is an arrogant young man.

MOORE, Mary. *Silver birch country.* London, Mills & Boon. 189p.
A girl returns to her small home town after visiting England.

MORRIESON, Ronald. *The predicament.* Palmerston North, Dunmore Press. 284p. Pages 7-12 contain information about the author by Maurice Shadbolt.
A teenage boy is involved in some extraordinary events in a small town.

OWEN, William. *Tryphena's summer.* Auckland, Collins. 326p.
About people living on isolated Great Barrier Island, 80 kilometres from Auckland, and the captain and crew of a scow that often berths there.

PFLAUM, Melanie (Lowenthal). *Lili, a novel.* Christchurch, Pegasus Press. 233p.
The life and loves of Lili and espionage in Germany and other places.

PHIPPS, Grace. *We love you Nurse Peters.* London, Hale. 192p.
A nurse is attracted to two doctors.

PRESTON, Ivy. *Romance in Glenmore Street.* London, Hale; Christchurch, Whitcombe & Tombs. 157p.
Four girls flatting together in Wellington.

PRESTON, Ivy. *Voyage of destiny.* London, Hale; Christchurch, Whitcombe & Tombs. 192p.
A romance with a variety of people on a ship proceeding from Auckland to England via the Panama Canal.

SCOTT, Mary. *It was meant*. London, Hurst & Blackett. 184p.
A New Zealand coach trip.

SHADBOLT, Maurice. *A touch of clay*. Auckland, Hodder & Stoughton. 190p.
After a failed marriage and a nervous breakdown, a lawyer turns to pottery and other diversions, including a new love with a young girl.

SUMMERS, Essie. *The gold of noon*. London, Mills & Boon. 222p.
A romance about a woman teacher in New Zealand and Austria.

SUMMERS, Essie. *Through all the years*. London, Mills & Boon. 191p.
A prize in a competition includes a trip to New Zealand.

SUTHERLAND, Margaret. *The Fledgling*. London, Heinemann. 175p.
A thirty-year-old spinster librarian becomes involved with the affairs of a young girl.

TAYLOR, William. *The chrysalis*. London, Hale. 190p.
A teacher at an intermediate school tries to sort out the problems of a part-Maori child.

1975

ANTHONY, Frank. *Follow the call*. With an unfinished novel entitled *Dave Baird*, edited and introduced by Terry Sturm. Auckland, Auckland University Press and O.U.P. xii, 148p. *Dave Baird* pages 111-138.
Two sheep farmers in a back country area after World War I.

BAGLEY, Desmond. *The snow tiger*. London, Collins. 287p.
An avalanche brings disaster to a small mining community.

BAKER, Herataunga Pananehu Pat. *Behind the tattooed face*. Whatamongo Bay, Cape Catley. 276p, glossary.
The first historical novel by a Maori writer. The setting is the Bay of Plenty and the novel depicts Maori inter-tribal wars. The marriage of a warrior chief and a princess brings peace.

BEVAN, Gloria. *Always a rainbow*. London, Mills & Boon. 188p.
A romance of a girl who is the cook for shearers on a sheep station.

BIANCHIN, Helen. *The willing heart*. London, Mills & Boon. 192p.
A romance in an Italian community set in Australia.

CLEARY, Frances. *A pocketful of years; another Mrs Kingi book*. London and Auckland, Collins. 166p. Sequel to *This Mrs Kingi*, 1971.
The book continues the story of rural life as seen by Mrs Kingi the Maori grandmother who exerts a maternal influence over countless people.

COWLEY, Joy. *The mandrake root*. Garden City, Doubleday. 309p.
Told in the first person by a troubled Elizabeth Stilwell whose well-known brother was killed in a car crash.

DAVIES, George Pearce. *Outback*. Palmerston North, Dunmore Press. 151p.
The novel is about an isolated farming community in the Marlborough Sounds.

DINGWELL, Joyce. *The kissing gate*. London, Mills & Boon. 186p.
Romance on Norfolk Island for a girl whose ancestors go back to the Pitcairners of the 'Bounty'.

DORMAN, Thomas Edwin. *The islander*. Auckland, Collins, 1974, i.e. 1975. 187p.
A Samoan comes to Auckland but discovers New Zealand is not a paradise and after involvement with crime returns home.

EDEN, Dorothy. *The time of the dragon*. London, Hodder & Stoughton. 255p.
An art dealer and his family in Peking at the time of the Boxer Rebellion.

HENDERSON, Michael Ronald. *The log of a superfluous son*. Dunedin, McIndoe. 143p.
On a freighter from New Zealand to Korea a man reviews his life.

LEE, John. *For mine is the kingdom*. Martinborough, Alister Taylor Publishing. 176p.
A study of Sir Ernest Booze, mayor of Auckland; politics; the liquor issue.

MACKRELL, Brian Heslop. *Only the land endures*. Auckland, Heinemann. 178p, frontispiece, maps, appendices pages 166-178.
The author, a diligent Maoriologist, describes cannibalistic wars in the 17th century around the Ruahine Ranges, and a high-born Maori girl's desire to marry a lowly suitor.

MARINER, David. *Symbol of vengeance*. London, Hale. 248p.
A thriller set in New Zealand and Antarctica includes a psychologist and a Russian glaciologist.

MITCALFE, Barry. *Moana...* Wellington, Seven Seas. 252p.
The title page carries the note: 'Moana is a true-to-life story of Maoris, whalers, convicts, missionaries and the impact of the first white men on New Zealand.' Moana is a Maori chief.

O'NEILL, David Patrick. *The book of Rewi; a utopian tale*. New York, Seabury Press (Continuum Books). 202p.
Six young people shipwrecked on an island in the South Pacific. The author is a New Zealand Roman Catholic priest.

PFLAUM, Melanie. *Safari*. Christchurch, Pegasus Press. 181p.
Several people on a safari in Africa with flashbacks to their lives. The author sometimes lives in New Zealand.

SANDERS, James. *Fire in the forest*. Wellington, Reed; published in association with Hale. 174p, glossary.
Historical novel of the Waikato war of the 1860s and a former American soldier searching for his half-caste wife and son.

SANDERS, James. *The lamps of Maine*. London, Hale. 168p.
A family on the coast of Maine during the war between England and America of 1812; includes whaling, fishing and naval warfare.

SANDERSON, Nora. *The sun breaks through*. London, Mills & Boon. 190p.
A romance in a rural area near Christchurch.

SCOTT, Mary. *Strangers for tea*. London, Hurst & Blackett. 184p.
A romance about a hitch-hiker.

SHADBOLT, Maurice. *Danger zone*. London, Auckland, Hodder & Stoughton. 206p.
The crew of a yacht sailing to the Mururoa atoll to protest against French atomic tests; the clashes of personality of those on board.

SUMMERS, Essie. *Anne of Strathallan*. London, Mills & Boon. 187p.
Romance on a sheep station in Otago.

TAYLOR, Brian. *The other shore*. Martinborough, Alister Taylor. 89p.
A ketch in the Pacific carries a minister of religion, an alcoholic, and her twin brother, an epileptic.

TEMPLE, Philip. *The explorer*. London, Auckland, Hodder & Stoughton. 143p.
Based on the life of Charles Edward Douglas (1840-1916), scientist, explorer and mountaineer. An ageing man accompanied by his dog, seeks a pass through the ranges of the West Coast of the South Island.

TOWNSHEND, Don J. *Gland time*. London, Collins. 256p.
Humorous tale set in Tasmania concerning a foreman in a freezing works and his loss of sexual innocence.

WATSON, Jean Catherine. *The balloon watchers*. Palmerston North, Dunmore Press. 97p.
A young girl finds happiness in a group with odd activities.

WORBOYS, Anne. *The lion of Delos*. London, Hodder & Stoughton, 218p.
Mystery and danger in Greece.

WORDSWORTH, Jane. *Reunion*. London, Hale; Christchurch, Whitcombe & Tombs. 191p.
A school reunion brings together pakeha and Maori, young and old. Race relations.

1976

BERG, Rilla. *Talisman for a bride*. London, Hale. 172p.
While an All Black is on tour the nurse to whom he is engaged falls in love with a doctor.

BEVAN, Gloria. *Dolphin Bay*. London, Mills & Boon. 189p.
A girl leaves England for New Zealand after a broken love affair.

BIANCIN, Helen. *Bewildered haven*. London, Mills & Boon. 188p.
A girl from Tauranga takes a position in Auckland with a legal firm.

CALDER, Jason. *The man who shot Rob Muldoon*. Palmerston North, Dunmore Press. 193p.
An attempt is made to assassinate New Zealand's Prime Minister.

FISHER, Bert. *Divers of Arakam*. Wellington, the author. 101p.
Some of the difficulties in making a living from fishing, including problems with the law.

FRANCIS, Dick. *In the frame*. London, Michael Joseph. 252p.
A thriller by an Australian writer set partly in New Zealand.

GANT, Phyllis. *The fifth season*. Auckland, Hodder & Stoughton. 145p.
A sympathetic woman and her boarder, a paranoid who is a cartoonist on the local paper.

GEE, Maurice. *Games of choice*. London, Faber. 171p.
Domestic problems of a man in a small seaside town with the generation gap causing strain.

HARRISON, Craig. *Broken October, New Zealand 1985*. Wellington, Reed. viii, 291p.
The author, an English immigrant, writes a forceful account of this country ten years hence with racial conflicts, terrorism and a Maori leading a group of revolutionaries.

JOSEPH, Michael. *A soldier's tale.* Auckland, Collins. 152p.
A harrowing weekend in Normandy in 1944 following the German evacuation; an English soldier's association with a woman who had consorted with German officers.

LANGFORD, Gary Raymond. *Death of the early morning hero.* Sydney, Angus & Robertson. 123p.
Described as a zany in love; the story is about an actor living in Sydney.

LEE, John. *Soldier.* Wellington, Reed. 148p.
World War I on the Western Front and in London with a partly autobiographical record of a young soldier who miraculously thwarted the obituary columns.

McLENAGHAN, Jack. *Travelling man.* Auckland, Collins. 186p.
Tough days in the depression with a man on the move taking on odd jobs where he can.

McLEOD, Rosemary. *A girl like I.* Dunedin, McIndoe. 126p, illustrations.
A satire on layabouts, women's lib and the indiscretions of a modern miss.

McNEISH, James Henry Peter. *The glass zoo.* London, Hodder & Stoughton. 350p.
A difficult fourteen-year-old boy at a comprehensive school in London.

MASON, Hugh. *The last enemy.* Armidale, NSW, Inchape Books. 187p.
A Sydney lecturer goes to New Zealand to escape his problems and assume a new identity.

MONCRIEFF, Perrine (Millais). *The rise and fall of David Riccio.* Wellington, Ambassador Publishing for the author. 191p.
An historical novel of the Italian musician who was secretary to Mary of Scotland.

MORRIESON, Ronald. *Pallet on the floor.* Palmerston North, Dunmore Press. 142p.
Life in a small town for a freezing works employee, his Maori wife and several other odd characters.

O'HAGAN, Joan. *Incline and fall; the death of Geoffrey Stretton.* London, Angus & Robertson. 222p.
Mystery surrounds the death of a young man at the New Zealand Migration Office in Rome.

O'SULLIVAN, Vincent Gerard. *Miracle; a romance.* Dunedin, McIndoe. 129p.
A satire on aspects of life in New Zealand, including rugby.

PEEL, Colin. *Flameout.* London, Hale. 191p.
A thriller which gives 'an account of one man's dangerous involvement in the West's frantic scramble for oil supplies' — dust cover.

PHIPPS, Grace. *Maternity hospital.* London, Hale. 160p.
A sister is uncertain which man to marry.

PRESTON, Ivy. *The house above the bay.* London, Hale. 152p.
What was the mystery behind the people in a South Island house that resembled a prison?

PRESTON, Ivy. *Moonlight on the lake.* London, Hale. 156p.
Two girls, cousins, come to New Zealand for a holiday at Lake Taupo.

SANDERS, James. *Where lies the land?* London, Hale. 174p.
Adventure for the 429 passengers on the immigrant ship Cospatrick *which left London in 1874; based on fact.*

SARGESON, Frank. *Sunset village.* Wellington, Reed. 91p.
The study of a diverse group of elderly, eccentric and suspicious occupants of some council flats who come under the close scrutiny of plain clothes detectives.

SUMMERS, Essie. *Not by appointment.* London, Mills & Boon. 186p.
Romance for a girl who accepts a housekeeping position with two orphaned children and their uncle.

SUTHERLAND, Margaret. *The love contract.* London, Heinemann. 227p.
Young married couple suffering from suburban blues with the pensive housewife seeking a more satisfying role in society.

WEDDE, Ian Curtis. *Dick Seddon's great dive; a novel.* In *Islands*, vol. 5 no. 2 1976, pages 117-212, published in Auckland. Also issued in hardcover edition of 200 copies.
A woman describes her attachment to a young man.

WILSON, Phillip. *Pacific star.* Wellington, Alister Taylor; London, Hale. Reissued in 1977 by the New English Library under the title *Kiwi strike.*
A New Zealand airman in the Pacific in World War II and his matrimonial problems.

1977

ABERDEIN, John Keith. *The governor.* Wellington, Hamlet Books. 304p.
Fictional biography based on a television series of Sir George Grey (1812-1898), Governor of New Zealand.

ANTHONY, Frank. *Gus Tomlins,* together with the original *Me and Gus,* edited and introduced by Terry Sturm. Auckland, Auckland University Press and O.U.P. xxii, 231p. *Gus Tomlins* here published for the first time pages 89-216.
There are comic situations when two former soldiers go dairy farming after World War I.

BERG, Rilla. *Legacy of thorns.* London, Hale. 189p.
Romance of a nurse who in taking over a case in isolated Taranaki is confronted with some odd situations.

BERG, Rilla. *An orchid for Belinda.* London, Hale. 192p.
Romance for Belinda Grant who takes up a nursing position near Taupo after returning from Britain.

BEVAN, Gloria. *Bachelor territory.* London, Mills & Boon. 187p.
A young woman is restless following the death of her foster parents.

BEVAN, Gloria. *Plantation moon.* London, Mills & Boon. 188p.
A girl leaves Auckland by plane for a Pacific island of which she has inherited a half share.

BIANCHIN, Helen S. *The hills of home.* London, Mills & Boon. 191p.
A romance set in Queensland where a girl goes home to visit her sick stepfather.

BIGGAR, Joan. *The maiden voyage.* Wellington, Reed; Glasgow, Molendinar Press. 156p.
Single girls leave Scotland for Port Chalmers in 1860.

BRITTON, Anna. *Fike's point.* London, Angus & Robertson. 148p.
A 14-year-old girl in an unstable family.

BRUCE, John Merlin Copplestone. *Airscream.* Auckland, Collins. 348p.
An air disaster and the subsequent enquiry turns a spotlight on many people and brings court action.

CALDER, Jason. *A wreath for the Springboks.* Palmerston North, Dunmore Press. 179p.
A thriller connected with race relations in New Zealand and a projected South African rugby football tour of the country.

CLAIR, Daphne. *Return to love.* London, Mills & Boon. 188p.
A girl returns to New Zealand and meets a man previously known to her.

DONALD, Robyn. *Bride at Whangatapu.* London, Mills & Boon. 188p.
A man wants to marry a woman to get possession of his son.

DRYLAND, Gordon. *Curious conscience.* Palmerston North, Dunmore Press. 190p.
Martin Baylis, a writer, reflects at forty on an unstable life.

EDEN, Dorothy. *The Salamanca drum.* London, Hodder & Stoughton. 284p.
Preoccupied with the military glory of her forbears, a woman is adamant that her sons become soldiers.

ELDRED-GRIGG, Stevan Treleaven. *Of ivory accents; a novel.* Hicksville, New York, Exposition Press. 48p.
A glimpse of an unsophisticated university student, his flatmate and his family.

FISHER, Bert. *Angels wear black; a novel.* Sequel to *Divers of Arakam,* 1976. Wellington, Mother Sea Publications. 113p, illustrations.
An uncertain future with terrorists, militia, depopulation and world government.

GEDGE, Pauline. *Child of the morning.* New York, Dial Press. 403p.
A study of Hatsheput, who was Queen of Egypt at the age of fifteen and ruled for two decades thirty-five centuries ago.

HAYTER, Adrian Goodenough. *A man called Peters.* Auckland, Hodder & Stoughton. 177p.
Hayter and his cobber return from World War II dissatisfied with politics and society. 'When the power of love overcomes the love of power, then there will be peace.'

JOSEPH, Michael. *The time of Achamoth.* Auckland and London, Collins. 181p.
Science fiction associated with time travel and a secret religious sect formulating the destruction of the world.

MARSH, Ngaio. *Last ditch.* London, Collins for the Crime Club. 277p.
The son of Chief Superintendent Alleyn goes to the Channel Islands over Easter to write a book.

MINCHER, Philip R. *The ride home; a story sequence.* Auckland, Longman Paul. 82p.
Roy and Kay are bikies who love the outdoor life.

PARK, Ruth. *Swords and crowns and rings.* Sydney, Thomas Nelson. 435p.
The characters include a dwarf in this story of two families in Australia during the depression of the 1930s.

PEEL, Colin. *Nightdive.* London, Hale. 173p.
A thriller.

PFLAUM, Melanie. *The old girls.* Christchurch, Pegasus. 335p.
The centenary celebrations of a United States girls' academy provide the opportunity to examine the lives of former students.

PRESTON, Ivy. *Sunlit seas.* London, Hale. 159p.
A romance set on a cruise ship in the Pacific.

PRIESTLEY, Clive Brian. *Makariri gold.* London, Macmillan. 191p.
Willy Rand's adventures in New Zealand begin when instead of meeting his brother he discovers a corpse.

SCOTT, Gavin. *Hot pursuit.* Auckland, Collins Crime Club. 193p.
A thriller set in New Zealand with the CIA and the KGB.

SCOTT, Mary. *Away from it all.* Auckland, Hurst & Blackett. 190p.
An author buries himself on a small farm.

SUMMERS, Essie. *Adair of Starlight Peaks.* London, Mills & Boon. 189p.
About a mother and daughter who paint for the tourist market in Otago and a man with property who should be married.

SUMMERS, Essie. *Goblin Hill.* London, Mills & Boon. 187p.
An adopted girl seeks to discover her father.

WENDT, Albert. *Pouliuli.* Auckland, Longman Paul. 147p, glossary.
The study of a chief and changing values in the old and the new Samoa.

WILSON, Trevor. *The newcomers.* London, Hale; Palmerston North, Dunmore Press. 174p.
Immigrants attracted to gold in Otago of the 1860s.

1978

BALLANTYNE, David. *The talk back man.* London, Hale. 222p.
A former Fleet Street journalist at an Auckland radio station has a Stir Line Show for listeners' complaints and is also occupied with hotel bars and women.

BERG, Rilla. *Decision for Nurse Lewis.* London, Hale. 192p.
A hospital romance.

BEVAN, Gloria. *Fringe of heaven.* London, Mills & Boon. 188p.
'Why should Christine right the situation between herself and Laurie Stuart, when that infuriating Kevin Hawke was going to misunderstand anything she did?' — advertisement.

BIANCHIN, Helen. *The vines in splendour.* London, Mills & Boon. 188p.
A romance set in the vineyards area near Auckland.

CALDER, Jason. *The O'Rourke affair.* London, Hale; Palmerston North, Dunmore Press. 203p.
A thriller about a private inquiry agent sent on a case from Australia to New Zealand.

CLAIR, Daphne. *The jade girl.* London, Mills & Boon. 187p.
A woman resents the man who takes an interest in her mother.

CLAIR, Daphne. *My darling Clementina.* London, Mills & Boon. 186p.
A girl goes to New Zealand and has difficulties with the man who wants to marry her.

CLAIR, Daphne. *A streak of gold.* London, Mills & Boon. 186p.
A woman meets a man she knew years before who has since married.

COWLEY, Joy. *The growing season.* New York, Doubleday. 208p.
The impending death of a dairy farmer provides the opportunity for a close study of him, his wife, his adult children and his brother.

CRAWFORD, James Temple. *The hot pick-up; a New Zealand mystery.* Morrinsville, Arrow Press. 173p.
An undercover detective is sent to the Coromandel area to investigate drug smuggling.

DONALD, Robyn. *Dilemma in paradise.* London, Mills & Boon. 189p.
A secretary engaged to her boss goes with him on a business trip to a South Pacific island.

DONALD, Robyn. *Summer at Awakopu.* London, Mills & Boon. 186p.
A girl who has just left school and is living by the sea in Northland meets a young man off a yacht.

DYKES, Mervyn Ian and Roger Simpson. *Gather your dreams.* Adapted by Mervyn Dykes from the television series by Roger Simpson. Auckland, Fontana/Collins. 123p.
The lives of theatre folk during the depression of the 1930s.

EWING, Barbara Jean. *Strangers.* Auckland, Heinemann. 131p.
A young Australian typist goes to England, attends a drama school and later becomes entangled in the anti-apartheid movement.

FISHER, Bert. *Dolphins and killer whales; a novel.* Wellington, Mother Sea Publications. 125p. Sequel to *Angels wear black* and the last of a trilogy.
Revolutionary methods are necessary to promote social justice.

GEE, Maurice. *Plumb.* London, Faber. 272p.
Covers in the first person with flashbacks the life of George Plumb, lawyer, parson, ex-parson and protester; and his numerous offspring. The novel has won several awards; the James Tait Black Memorial Prize for the best novel in Great Britain; the New Zealand Book Award for prose fiction; the Buckland Literary Award for a New Zealand work of the highest literary merit.

GLOVER, Denis. *Men of God.* Illustrations by Peter Watson. Palmerston North, Dunmore Press. 125p.
Three men of the church, Presbyterian, Anglican and Roman Catholic, cooperate in a monster gala with assistance from a good-natured and previously incarcerated scrounger.

GRACE, Patricia Frances. *Mutuwhenua; the moon sleeps.* Auckland, Longman Paul. 155p.
A Maori girl tells of her love for a pakeha school teacher against the opposition of her grandmother. After marriage and the move into the pakeha world she discovers the strength of the old Maori customs.

HEATH, Michael. *Solo; a love story of our time.* Sydney, Horowitz. 125p. Based on the screenplay of Tony Williams and Martyn Sanderson.
A romance involving a forestry pilot with a twelve-year-old son and a girl tramper.

HILLIARD, Noel. *The glory and the dream.* Auckland, Heinemann. 260p. Sequel to *Maori woman* (1974); completes the Netta Samuel tetralogy; *Maori girl* (1960), *Power of joy* (1965). *The author explores the relationship between a white husband and his Maori spouse; its conflicts, joys and compromises when tensions are increased by the arrival of their first child.*

LAY, Graeme John. *The mentor.* Whatamongo Bay, Cape Catley. vii, 179p.
A thriller of the contemporary New Zealand literary scene; a teacher who wants to write and his association with an older man of letters.

MANTELL, Lorraine (Laurie Mantell). *Murder in fancy dress.* London, Gollancz. 190p.
The holiday spirit at Petone with its wild west show is shattered with the death of a constable.

MARSH, Ngaio. *Grave mistake.* London, Collins. 278p.
Sleuths Alleyn and Fox investigate the death of the Hon. Mrs Sybil Foster, a wealthy hypochondriac.

MITCHELL, June Ellis. *Amokura.* Auckland, Longman Paul. xi, 204p, maps, glossary.
History, biography and fiction permeate this work which records the life of Te Akau Horohau, known as Meretini after marrying Thomas Uppandine Cook in 1842; the title is the name of a greenstone mere. 'I have tried to let a Maori voice speak to us from her pathway through the nineteenth century.' — the author.

PEEL, Colin. *Hell seed.* London, Hale. 190p.
A thriller.

PHIPPS, Grace. *A doctor like Ross.* London, Hale. 159p.
A doctor in love with a patient's daughter.

PRIESTLEY, Brian. *The island emperor.* London, Macmillan. 189p.
A sequel to Makariri gold *(1977). Told by Colonel Willy Rand, this thriller is set in the South Pacific.*

ROBERTSON, J. R. *The crab eagle trees.* London, Hale. 157p.
Science fiction about a couple in the Bay of Islands and the destructive multiplying of crab eagles.

SANDERS, James. *Chase the dragon.* London, Hale. 192p.
A mystery thriller set in South-East Asia where an English woman is entrusted with an important package.

SANDYS, Elspeth. *Catch a falling star.* London, Blond & Briggs. 351p.
Based on the Elizabethan poet John Donne.

SAUNDERS, G. K. *The stranger.* Sydney, Whitcombe & Tombs. 217p.
Visitors from another world make secret visits to the planet Earth. Based on a radio and television series.

SCOTT, Mary. *Board but no breakfast.* Auckland, Hutchinson. 184p.
More of the lives of Susan and Larry and their tenants in holiday homes; the author's last novel before she died on 16 July, 1979.

SLIGO, John. *The cave; a novel.* Dunedin, John McIndoe, 80p.
Described as a story of human bondage and bestiality and a search for justice and truth.

SPENCER, Earle. *Moynihan: the set up.* Palmerston North, Dunmore Press. 260p, illustrations.
Continues the story of the television series Moynihan, *about a trade union official, industry and the government; set in Wellington.*

SUMMERS, Essie. *The lake of the kingfisher.* London, Mills & Boon. 187p.
A young woman returns to Otago from overseas to redecorate an old homestead.

SUMMERS, Essie. *Spring in September.* London, Mills & Boon. 187p.
A girl is in a quandary over two attractive men.

SUTHERLAND, James Hector. *The elver.* Morrinsville, J. Sutherland. 87p, illustrations.
A ten-year-old boy shattered by the death of a friend goes to stay on his uncle's farm to recover from the ordeal.

WATSON, Jean Catherine. *The world is an orange and the sun.* Palmerston North, Dunmore Press. 185p.
A young housewife living in the country records the life of her family and neighbours.

1979

BERG, Rilla. *Dr Herbert's dilemma.* London, Mills & Boon. 191p.
Romance in the South Island.

BIANCHIN, Helen. *Edge of spring.* London, Mills & Boon. 187p.
After a brief marriage a woman moves to Auckland to begin a new life.

BIANCHIN, Helen. *Stormy possession.* London, Mills & Boon. 187p.
To marry or allow her father to go bankrupt was a young girl's difficult choice.

CAMPION, Edith. *The chain.* In *Tandem,* pages 1-79.
Fictional reconstruction of the true story of a man who was left in the bush chained to a tree.

CLAIR, Daphne. *The jasmine bride.* London, Mills & Boon. 187p.
An inexperienced girl is married to an older, sophisticated man.

CLAIR, Daphne. *The sleeping fire.* London, Mills & Boon. 191p.
The woman editor of Lively Lady *is apprehensive about a new staff member who makes a number of changes.*

CLAIR, Daphne. *Something less than love.* London, Mills & Boon. 188p.
Following his discharge from hospital, a man is a worry to his young wife.

DONALD, Robyn. *Shadow of the past.* London, Mills & Boon. 187p.
A Karitane nurse returns to Northland and is embarrassed by the attentions of the brother of a former boy friend.

DONALD, Robyn. *Wife in exchange.* London, Mills & Boon. 188p.
A romance of a New Zealand girl on a Pacific island.

EDEN, Dorothy. *The Storrington papers.* London, Hodder & Stoughton. 221p.
A woman is engaged as a private secretary to assist in the compilation of a family history.

FRAME, Janet. *Living in the Maniototo.* New York, Braziller. 240p.
Strange characters and situations with elements of fantasy in a work set in New Zealand and the United States. The Maori word in the title means 'bloody plain'.

GRAY, Alison Margaret. *The marriage maze.* Whatamongo Bay, Cape Catley. 155p.
An account of an unhappy modern marriage of two university students with an emphasis on the woman's difficulties.

HOLMES, Robert Barry. *The Elizabeth affair.* London, Hale; Palmerston North, Dunmore Press. 190p.
The Elizabeth *is a brig under Captain Stewart who has trouble with his crew in New Zealand waters in the 1830s.*

HOOPER, Peter. *A song in the forest.* Illustrations by Chris Gaskin. Dunedin, McIndoe. 218p.
The youth Tama, following an excursion to the east coast of the South Island centuries hence, brings change to his tribe in Westland.

JOSEPH, George. *Trial and error.* London, Hale; Christchurch, Whitcoulls. 239p.
The author, a lawyer, writes of a murder trial where a barrister becomes emotionally involved in the defence of his client.

KIDMAN, Fiona Judith. *A breed of women.* Sydney, Harper & Row. 345p.
The life of Harriet Wallace from adolescence on the farm to her success in television.

LANGFORD, Gary. *Players in the ball game.* Melbourne, Macmillan. 169p.
A frank study of a school teacher artist and his ladies.

MANSFIELD, Katherine. *Maata.* Edited by Margaret Scott. In The Turnbull Library record, vol. 12 no. 1 May 1979 pages 10-28. See also *The mystery of Maata, a Katherine Mansfield novel,* by P. A. Lawlor, with an introduction by G. H. Scholefield. Wellington, The Beltane Book Bureau, 1946. 39p, portrait.
An outline of 35 chapters of her 1913 projected novel plus the two opening chapters.

MIDDLETON, Ian. *Pet shop.* Martinborough, Alister Taylor. 208p.
A boy moves from a rural area to work in the city and later is on a tanker during World War II.

MIDDLETON, Osman Edward. *Confessions of an ocelot.* Dunedin, McIndoe. 63p.
A young man interested in music and literature; his friendship with a slightly older man.

PARVIN, Brian. *The deadly dyke*. London, Hale.
157p.
A thriller.

POWELL, John D. *Silent knife*. London, Hale;
Palmerston North, Dunmore Press. 189p.
*The puzzling deaths of former New Zealand soldiers
many years after World War II.*

PRESTON, Ivy. *One broken dream*. London, Hale.
160p.
*A nurse in love with a doctor is disconsolate when he
is attracted to her older sister.*

SARGESON, Frank. *En route*. In *Tandem*,
Wellington, Reed, pages 83-168.
*A tale of two women and the daughter of one of them
in a rural area.*

SIMONS, Wendy. *Harper's mother*. London, Angus
& Robertson. 190p.
*Harper O'Leary, an observant teenager, tells the story
of life with her solo mother, and the variety of
their domestic experiences.*

STEVENS, David. *White for danger*. London,
Collins. 221p, map.
*Adventure and mystery in Antarctica with a group of
men and a woman seeking explanations of a lost
city and missing men.*

SUMMERS, Essie. *My lady of the fuchsias*. London,
Mills & Boon. 188p.
*A girl relinquishes her job because she is in love with
her boss who is engaged to someone else.*

SUMMERS, Essie. *One more river to cross*. London,
Mills & Boon. 188p.
*A romance involving two girls who resemble each
other but are of very different temperaments.*

TEMPLE, Philip. *Stations*. Auckland, Collins. 216p.
*Pioneer life as experienced by a Scottish couple who
establish through great hardship a sheep station near
the Southern Alps.*

TRAVIS, Neal. *Manhattan*. New York, Crown. 250p.
*The title is the name of a trendy New York magazine
and the novel is a mixture of sex, money, power and
crime.*

WENDT, Albert. *Leaves of the Banyan Tree*.
Auckland, Longman Paul. 413p, glossary.
*A comprehensive study covering half a century of a
Samoan family and community with its rich, powerful
and feared leader and the changes wrought by contact
with Europeans.*

WILLIAMS, Robert J. *Skin deep*. Wellington, Reed.
194p.
*Reactions in a small North Island town when a
massage parlour is opened. Adapted from the feature
film* Skin Deep, *1979.*

WILSON, Trevor. *Yellow fever*. London, Hale;
Palmerston North, Dunmore Press. 190p. Sequel
to *The newcomers*, 1977.
*English immigrants in the 1860s face innumerable
hardships when lured by the gold at Gabriel's Gully.*

Title Index

The date shown refers to the year under which the novel is included in the bibliography.

Absence of angels, An. Dryland, G. 1965
Across two seas. Forde, H. 1896
Adair of Starlight Peaks. Summers, E. 1977
Adaptable man, The. Frame, J. 1965
Adapted to stress. Peel, C. 1973
Adopted family, The. Peacocke, I. 1923
Adrift in the Pacific. Verne, J. 1888
Adventures of George Washington Pratt, The. Pyke, V. 1874
Affair of men, An. Brathwaite, E. 1961
After Anzac Day. Cross, I. 1961
Airscream. Bruce, J. 1977
Alice Lauder. Wilson, A. 1893
Allen Adair. Mander, J. 1925
Along the ribbonwood track. Moore, M. 1971
Along the road. Bacon, R. 1964
Alpha trip, The. Billing, G. 1968
Altar stairs, The. Lyttleton, E. 1908
Always a rainbow. Bevan, G. 1975
Amanda. Mackay, M. 1963
Ambition's harvest. Scanlan, N. 1935
Amokura. Mitchell, J. 1978
Among the cannibals. Verne, J. 1868
Among the cinders. Shadbolt, M. 1965
Amongst the Maoris. Marryatt, E. 1874
Anchorage, The. Koebel, W. 1908
And be my love. Phipps, G. 1972
And shadows flee. Scott, M. 1935
Angel in the coffin, The. Ellis, M. 1960
Angel Isafrel, The. Reed, G. 1896
Angels wear black. Fisher, B. 1977
Anna of Strathallan. Summers, E. 1975
Anno Domini 2000. Vogel, J. 1889
Another man's role. Grover, R. 1967
Any old dollars, Mister? Harvey, B. 1963
Anzac's bride, An. Gibbons, M. 1918
April in Westland. Preston, I. 1969
April's sowing. Rees, R. 1924
Artists in crime. Marsh, N. 1938
As short a spring. Casey, R. 1963
Ask the river. Peters, C. 1964
At the front. Foston, H. 1921
Atareta. Grace, A. 1908
Away from it all. Scott, M. 1977

Bachelor territory. Bevan, G. 1977
Backward sex, The. Cross, I. 1960
Balloon watchers, The. Watson, J. 1975
Balloons. Dryland, G. 1973
Barbarous tongue, A. Duckworth, M. 1963
Barrier, The. Hughes, I. 1968
Bay of the nightingales, The. Summers, E. 1970
Behind closed doors. Clarke, N. 1964
Behind the tattooed face. Baker, H. 1975
Bell call. Ashton-Warner, S. 1964
Bella. Eden, D. 1964
Beneath the thunder. Wilson, P. 1963
Besieging city, The. Mander, J. 1926
Better to trust. Rees, R. 1956
Beware my heart. Fenton, E. 1957
Beware of the dawn. Lindsay, K. 1959
Beyond the breakers. Holcroft, M. 1928
Beyond the ranges. Bevan, G. 1970
Big one, The. Peters, C. 1963
Big season, The. Gee, M. 1962
Bird in the chimney, The. Eden, D. 1963
Bird in the wilderness. Brent, M. 1961
Birds of time. Addison, D. 1965
Bitter autumn. Peel, C. 1973
Black as he's painted. Marsh, N. 1974
Black noon at Ngutu. St. Bruno, A. 1960
Blue gum tree, The. Quentin, D. 1953
Blue Pheasant, The. Boswell, J. 1958
Blue remembered hills, The. Preston, I. 1965
Board but no breakfast. Scott, M. 1978
Body in my arms. Stephenson, R. 1963
Bonzer Jones. Smyth, W. 1929
Book of Rewi, The. O'Neill, D. 1975
Boy on the mountain. Rooke, D. 1969
Brave company. Wilson, G. 1950
Brazilian daughter. Holcroft, M. 1931
Breakfast at six. Scott, M. 1953
Breed of women, A. Kidman, F. 1979
Bridal boutique, The. Phipps, G. 1971
Bride at Whangatapu. Donald, R. 1977
Bride by candlelight. Eden, D. 1954
Bride in flight. Summers, E. 1964
Brides of price. Davin, D. 1972
Broad stairway, The. Carman, D. 1924

Edge of spring. Bianchin, H. 1979
Edge of the alphabet, The. Frame, J. 1962
Elixir of life, The. Satchell, W. 1907
Elizabeth affair, The. Holmes, R. 1979
Elver, The. Sutherland, J. 1978
Emma. Kenyon, F. 1955
Empty hills, The. Holden, A. 1967
En route. Sargeson, F. 1979
Ena. Wilson, G. 1874
Enter a murderer. Marsh, N. 1935
Episode. Taylor, W. 1970
Erewhon. Butler, S. 1872
Erewhon revisited. Butler, S. 1901
Errand of mercy. Quentin, D. 1941
Eve Stanley of New Zealand. Deverell, E. 1909
Eve's own Eden. Mutch, K. 1971
Everything is possible to will. Ellis, E. 1882
Evil day, The. Brathwaite, E. 1967
Exit with emeralds. Andrews, I. 1971
Expedition of Captain Flick, The. Hume, F. 1896
Explorer, The. Temple, P. 1975

Faces in the water. Frame, J. 1961
Faces of love, The. House, L. 1964
Failed to pass. Shortland, E. 1885
Falcon rising, A. Hughes, I. 1966
False dawn, The. Carman, D. 1962
False scent. Marsh, N. 1959
Families are fun. Scott, M. 1956
Family affair, A. Hill, J. 1963
Fanned flame, The. Winder, M. 1968
Far flung. Cook, H. 1925
Far from the sun. Ewen, J. 1966
Farewell to a valley. Grayland, V. 1971
Fatal lady. Scott, M. 1960
Fear in the night. Brathwaite, E. 1959
Feared and the fearless, The. Wilson, G. 1954
Fifth season, The. Gant, P. 1976
Figures in light. Shadbolt, M. 1967
Fike's point. Britton, A. 1977
Final curtain. Marsh, N. 1947
Fingal's box. Williams, H. 1941
Fire in the forest. Sanders, J. 1975
Fires in the distance. Courage, J. 1952
First things first. Scott, M. 1973
Flame in Fiji. Bevan, G. 1973
Flame of Ethirdova, The. Bolitho, H. 1930
Flameless fire, The. Holcroft, M. 1929
Flameout. Peel, C. 1976
Fledgling, The. Sutherland, M. 1974
Fleeting breath, A. Preston, I. 1970
Flower of delight. Dorien, R. 1956
Fly away dove. McCarthy, C. 1956
Fly away Peter. Rhodes, D. 1952
Flying fish, The. Brathwaite, E. 1964
Follow a shadow. Reyburn, W. 1956
Follow, follow. Glenday, A. 1973

Follow the call. Anthony, F. 1936
Folly is joy. Winder, M. 1973
Fool's gold. Mason, H. 1960
Footsteps in the sea. Booth, P. 1964
For mine is the kingdom. Lee, J. 1975
For the rest of our lives. Davin, D. 1947
Forbidden gold. Lawson, W. 1946
Forbidden marriage. Hutchinson, I. 1971
Forbidden valley, The. Summers, E. 1973
Forbush and the penguins. Billing, G. 1965
Forgotten heritage. Staples, M. 1966
Forsaken orchard, The. Jeffery, M. 1955
Fortunately there was a haystack. McLeod, C. 1970
Four women. Wordsworth, J. 1972
Fourth point of the star, The. Walsh, H. 1947
Frank Melton's luck. Cottle, T. 1891
Fred. Crump, B. 1972
Freddie. Scott, M. 1965
Fresh and the salt, The. Stringfellow, O. 1959
Friend of the family, A. Ballantyne, D. 1966
Fringe of heaven. Bevan, G. 1978
From the south. Ritchie, K. 1972
Frost and the fire, The. Park, R. 1957
Fugitive from fear. Wilson, T. 1972
Furious masters, The. Bennett, M. 1968
Fury at Finnegan's Folly. St. Bruno, A. 1962

Gallows tree, A. Preston, F. 1956
Game of hide and seek, A. Sargeson, F. 1972
Games of choice. Gee, M. 1976
Gap in the spectrum, A. Duckworth, M. 1959
Gather your dreams. Dykes, M. 1978
Gay pretensions, The. Preston, F. 1959
Generous heart, The. Quentin, D. 1955
Girl like I, A. McLeod, R. 1976
Girl on the beach, The. Holden, A. 1973
Give them swing bands. Burfield, E. 1969
Gland time. Townshend, D. 1975
Glass sharp and poisonous. Gilbert, G. 1952
Glass zoo, The. McNeish, J. 1976
Glitter and the gold, The. Winder, M. 1967
Glitter not the gold, The. Berg, R. 1974
Glory and the dream, The. Hilliard, N. 1978
Glowing dark, The. McGregor, M. 1968
Goblin Hill. Summers, E. 1977
God boy, The. Cross, I. 1957
God killers, The. Journet, T. 1968
Godwits fly, The. Hyde, R. 1938
Gold in their hearts. Lawson, W. 1951
Gold of noon, The. Summers, E. 1974
Golden dawns the sun. Messenger, E. 1962
Goldenhaze. Quentin, D. 1969
Golden hibiscus, The. Quentin, D. 1949
Good and evil. Reyburn, W. 1962
Good and faithful servant. Maughan, C. 1974
Good keen girl, A. Crump, B. 1970
Good keen man, A. Crump, B. 1960

Jem Peterkin's daughter. Churchward, W. 1892
Jennifer Grant, New Zealand nurse. Holt, S. 1965
Jest of darkness. Grayland, V. 1965
Johnny Rapana. Peters, C. 1964
Journey into twilight. Guthrie, J. 1949
Journey to New Zealand. Hansen, O. 1935
Joy of the worm. Sargeson, F. 1969
Judith Silver. Bolitho, H. 1929
Julia. Luson, P. 1971
Julia Deverell. Hughes, I. 1962
Julien Ware. Wilson, G. 1952

Kath. Henshaw, W. 1964
Kauri hill. Lord, A. 1957
Kelly Pencarrow. Scanlan, N. 1939
Killer Dolphin. Marsh, N. 1966
Killing of Jacqueline Love, The. Devanny, J. 1942
Kind of treason, A. Bates, P. 1973
Kindled fire, The. Summers, E. 1969
Kindred of the winds. Sanders, J. 1973
Kissing gate, The. Dingwell, J. 1975
Kit Carmichael. Scanlan, N. 1946
Kiwi strike. Wilson, P. 1976
Knock softly on death's door. Wilson, T. 1971
Ko Meri. Weston, J. 1890

Lady had a tiger, The. Brodie, G. 1968
Lady of the heather, The. Lawson, W. 1945
Lake of enchantment, The. Rees, R. 1925
Lake of the kingfisher, The. Summers, E. 1978
Lamb to the slaughter. Eden, E. 1953
Lamp in the window, The. Winder, M. 1969
Lamps of Maine, The. Sanders, J. 1975
Lancet and the land, The. Scott, N. 1966
Land of my children. Wilson, H. 1955
Land of the lost, The. Satchell, W. 1902
Landscape with figures. Mulcock, A. 1971
Language of love. Wylie, C. 1966
Lark in the meadow, The. Summers, E. 1959
Larks in cages. Hurne, R. 1963
Last ditch. Marsh, N. 1977
Last enemy, The. Mason, H. 1976
Last pioneer, The. Ballantyne, D. 1963
Lauder brothers, New Zealand, The. Clapperton, A. 1936
Leave me in the park. Adsett, D. 1974
Leaves of the banyan tree. Wendt, A. 1979
Legacy of thorns. Berg, R. 1977
Leisure for living. Scanlan, N. 1937
Lenore Divine. Devanny, J. 1926
Lie fallow my acre. Joseph, G. 1957
'Life's what you make it.' Rees, R. 1927
Light on murder. Messenger, E. 1960
Lili. Pflaume, M. 1974
Limanora. Brown, J. 1903
Lineman's ticket. Gilbert, M. 1967
Lion of Delos, The. Worboys, A. 1975
Listening in the music place. Rawlinson, G. 1938

Little country, The. Guthrie, J. 1935
Little millstones, The. Worboys, A. 1970
Living in the Maniototo. Frame, J. 1979
Log of a superfluous son, The. Henderson, M. 1975
London called them. Peacocke, I. 1946
Long honeymoon, The. Scott, M. 1963
Long night among the stars. Booth, P. 1961
Long night's journey. Mackersey, I. 1974
Long vacation, A. Verne, J. 1888
Long way home. Brathwaite, E. 1964
Long white cloud, The. Archibald, M. 1963
Long White Cloud, The. Rogers, R. 1960
Long winter, The. Burfield, E. 1964
Lost at the gold fields. Pyke, V. 1868
Love contract, The. Sutherland, M. 1976
Love is vanity. Mountain, J. 1948
Love-keeper, The. Gibson, C. 1970
Love keeps no score. Winder, M. 1964
Loves of Dretta Gray, The. O'Sullivan, K. 1948
Luck of the islands. Brown, J. 1963

Maata. Mansfield, K. 1979
McDunnit dunnit. Crump, W. 1964
McGlusky's great adventure. Hales, A. 1917
Mackenzie. McNeish, J. 1970
Macpherson's Gully. Wardon, R. 1892
Magic in Maoriland. Preston, I. 1962
Magpie sings, A. Adsett, D. 1963
Maiden voyage, The. Biggar, J. 1977
Mairangi. Jeffery, M. 1964
Makariri gold. Priestley, C. 1977
Make way for tomorrow. Bevan, G. 1971
Making his pile. MacCartie, J. 1891
Makutu. Davis, T. 1960
Man alone. Mulgan, J. 1939
Man called Peters, A. Hayter, A. 1977
Man lay dead, A. Marsh, N. 1934
Man of England now. Sargeson, F. 1972
Man of straw. Cowley, J. 1970
Man out of mind. Bates, P. 1968
Man who gave, The. Thomas, W. 1963
Man who guided missiles, The. Denman, P. 1973
Man who shot Rob Muldoon, The. Calder, J. 1976
Mana. Jackson, L. 1969
Mandarin's way. Kelly, M. 1972
Mandrake root, The. Cowley, J. 1975
Mangrove murder, The. Scott, M. 1963
Manhattan. Travis, N. 1979
Manuka fire. Moore, M. 1974
Maori and settler. Henty, G. 1890
Maori gateway, The. Carman, D. 1963
Maori girl. Hilliard, N. 1960
Maori Jack's monster. Crisp, F. 1956
Maori maid, A. Vogel, H. 1898
Maori witchery. Browne, C. 1929
Maori woman. Hilliard, N. 1970
Mara. Addison, D. 1964
Marana. Sutton, P. 1958

March moon. Scanlan, N. 1944
March of the little men. Bennett, F. 1971
Marie Levant. Ferguson, C. 1913
Mark Anderson. Langton, W. 1889
Marriage chest, The. Eden, D. 1965
Marriage maze, The. Gray, A. 1979
Marriage of Nicholas Cotter, The. Scanlan, N. 1936
Marriage with Eve. Phipps, G. 1955
Martin Tobin. Campbell, Lady. 1864
Mary Bravender. Stringfellow, O. 1959
Mary Smith's Hotel. Lawson, W. 1951
Mask of the clown, The. Taylor, W. 1970
Matai Valley magic. Moore, M. 1973
Match-box house, The. Duckworth, M. 1960
Material witness. Messenger, E. 1959
Maternity hospital. Phipps, G. 1976
Mates. Ferguson, D. 1912
Me and Gus. Anthony, F. 1938, 1951
Me and Gus again. Anthony, F. 1955
Men of God. Glover, D. 1978
Mentor, The. Lay, G. 1978
Mercia Wade. Baume, E. 1947
Merciless, The. Nethercote, R. 1970
Merry-go-round. Guthrie, J. 1950
Merry marauders, The. Rees, A. 1913
Memoirs of a peon. Sargeson, F. 1965
Memory's yoke. Winder, M. 1962
Midnight sea, The. Cameron, I. 1958
Mihawhenua. Chapman, R. 1888
Millionaire's daughter, The. Eden, D. 1974
Miracle. O'Sullivan, V. 1976
Miracle of Tane, The. Carman, D. 1962
Miranda Stanhope. Mactier, S. 1911
Mirror image. Prior, A. 1969
Miss Tiverton's shipwreck. Rees, R. 1936
Mister. Burgess, M. 1964
Mr Oseba's last discovery. Bell, G. 1904
Mrs Nelly. Kenyon, F. 1961
Moana. Mitcalfe, B. 1975
Mocking shadows. Staples, M. 1941
Monday at McMurdo. Burke, D. 1967
Month of the brittle star, The. Soper, E. 1971
Moonlight on the lake. Preston, I. 1976
Moonshine. Wilson, H. 1944
Moral issues here and abroad. Gee, W. 1964
More me and Gus. Anthony, F. 1952
Morning tide. Addison, D. 1967
Mortal sin of Father Grossard, The. Baume, F. 1953
Mountains are still green, The. Quentin, D. 1950
Moving target. McClenaghan, J. 1966
Moynihan. Spencer, E. 1978
Multiple texture, A. Dryland, G. 1973
Murder by court martial. Lambe, Z. 1967
Murder in fancy dress. Mantell, L. 1978
Murder stalks the bay. Messenger, E. 1958
Mussolini's millions. Lee, J. 1970
Mutton on the menu. Davis, M. 1962
Mutuwhenua. Grace, P. 1978

My dangerous love. Helliwell, A. 1974
My darling Clementina. Clair, D. 1978
My lady of the fuchsias. Summers, E. 1979
Myola. Musgrove, H. 1917

Naked under Capricorn. Ruben, O. 1958
Naked we are born. Carrel, V. 1960
Narrative of Edward Crewe, The. Baines, W. 1874
Neath the Maori moon. Carman, D. 1948
Necklace of El-Hoya, The. Carman, D. 1967
Needle's eye, The. Brathwaite, E. 1965
Nest in a falling tree. Cowley, J. 1967
Never call it loving. Eden, D. 1966
New gate for Mattie Dulivich, A. Audley, E. 1965
New Zealand calling. Smith, H. 1936
New Zealand inheritance. Summers, E. 1957
New Zealand Jack. Wilson, P. 1973
New Zealand pearl, A. Stelin, E. 1896
New Zealander, The. Dingwell, J. 1963
Newcomers, The. Wilson, T. 1977
Ngamihi. Scott, R. 1895
Nice day for murder, A. Bevan, G. 1971
Night at Green River, A. Hilliard, N. 1969
Night at the Vulcan. Marsh, N. 1951
Nightdive. Peel, C. 1977
Night of the reaper. Grayland, V. 1963
No bells were ringing. Sanderson, N. 1968
No boots for Mr Moehau. Audley, E. 1963
No easy answer. Smith, M. 1962
No humour in my love. (Solemn boy.) Bolitho, H. 1946
No red herrings. Scott, M. 1964
'No reference intended.' Crump, B. 1971
No remittance. Davin, D. 1959
No sad songs. Scott, M. 1960
No saints on this highway. Mutch, K. 1971
No welcome for Nurse Jane. Sanderson, N. 1968
No wife for a parson. Phipps, G. 1969
Nor the years condemn. Hyde, R. 1938
Not by appointment. Summers, E. 1976
Not here, not now. Davin, D. 1970
Now and forever. Hoare, H. 1973
Nurse like Kate, A. Phipps, G. 1963
Nursing home murder, The. Marsh, N. 1935

O kiss me Kate. Thian, V. 1970
Oak uprooted. Wright, S. 1936
Obsession. Gurr, T. 1958
Odd spot of bother, The. Crump, B. 1967
Of ivory accents. Eldred-Grigg, S. 1977
Of men and angels. Cowley, J. 1972
Off with his head. Marsh, N. 1956
Old girls, The. Pflaum, M. 1977
Old men are fools. Bates, P. 1970
One-a-pecker, two-a-pecker. Park, R. 1957
One broken dream. Preston, I. 1979
One house. Courage, J. 1933
One more river to cross. Summer, E. 1979
One of us. Crump, B. 1962

Riven. Devanny, J. 1929
Road the men came home, The. Hunter, E. 1920
Roads from home. Davin, D. 1949
Rolling stone, A. Cheesman, C. 1886
Romance for Judith. Swift, R. 1971
Romance in Glenmore Street. Preston, I. 1974
Rosalind comes home. Summers, E. 1968
Rusty road, The. Scanlan, N. 1948

Safari. Pflaum, M. 1975
Sailin' down the Clyde. Griffin, A. 1961
Sails of destiny. McGregor, M. 1971
Salamanca drum, The. Eden, D. 1977
Sane Jane. Rees, R. 1931
Scales of justice. Marsh, N. 1955
Scan the dark coast. Ruhen, O. 1969
Scapegoat, The. Davis, G. 1974
Scarecrow, The. Morrieson, J. 1963
Scene is changed, The. Ray, J. 1932
Scent of the woods. Winder, M. 1965
Scented gardens for the blind. Frame, J. 1963
Schoolmaster's daughters, The. Eden, D. 1948
Schooner came to Atia, The. Finlayson, R. 1953
Score at tea-time, The. Ellis, M. 1957
Scrapwaggon. Crump, B. 1965
Seal woman. Lockley, R. 1974
Season at Sunrise, The. Michael, S. 1970
Second romance. Rees, R. 1931
Seekers, The. Guthrie, J. 1952
Seventeen come Sunday. Garford, J. 1961
Shadow of Hilton Fernbrook, The. Westbury, F. 1896
Shadow of the land, The. Houghton, P. 1966
Shadow of the past. Donald, R. 1979
Shadowed journey. Winder, M. 1955
Shadows in the ward. Sanderson, N. 1964
Shadows on the snow. Farjeon, B. 1865
Shallow end, The. Penberthy, B. 1972
Share milkers, The. Thompson, N. 1966
Sheep kings, The. West, J. 1936
Sheep thief. Newton, P. 1972
Shepherd's pie. Scott, M. 1972
She's right. Cathie, D. 1953
Shifter, The. Platts, H. 1911
Shiner Slattery. Lee, J. 1964
Shining with the Shiner. Lee, J. 1944
Ships of Tarshish, The. Fairburn, E. 1867
Shores of wrath, The. Sanders, J. 1972
Short madness, The. Manning, A. 1960
Show down. Escott, M. 1936
Sigh for Selina. Brent, M. 1970
Silent knife. Powell, J. 1979
Silent mountain, The. Mann, C. 1955
Silver birch country. Moore, M. 1974
Sing a song of Sydney. Rees, R. 1938
Singing in the shrouds. Marsh, N. 1958
Singing shadows. Eden, D. 1940
Singing water, The. Hughes, I. 1963
Skin deep. Williams, R. 1979

Sleep in the woods. Eden, D. 1960
Sleepers can kill. Jay, S. 1968
Sleeping fire, The. Clair, D. 1979
Slipway, The. Billing, G. 1973
Smiling house, The. Grayland, V. 1973
Smith's dream. Stead, C. 1971
Smoke and the fire, The. Summers, E. 1964
Smokers of hashish, The. Berrow, N. 1934
Snow man. Hogg, J. 1934
Snow tiger, The. Bagley, D. 1975
So they began. Guthrie, J. 1936
Soldier. Lee, J. 1976
Soldier's tale, A. Joseph, M. 1976
Solemn boy. Bolitho, H. 1927
Solo. Heath, M. 1978
Something in the country air. Grieve, H. 1947
Something less than love. Clair, D. 1979
Son of Peter. Lloyd, V. 1930
Song in the forest, A. Hooper, P. 1979
Sons for the return home. Wendt, A. 1973
Sophisticated urchin, The. Henaghan, R. 1970
South Sea siren, A. Chamier, G. 1895
South to forget. Summers, E. 1963
Speak to me of love. Eden, D. 1972
Special flower, A. Gee, M. 1965
Spinster. Ashton-Warner, S. 1958
Spinsters in jeopardy. Marsh, N. 1953
Splendid horizon, The. Greenwood, H. 1931
Spring in September. Summers, E. 1978
Spring in the bishop's palace. Bliss, A. 1969
Spring manoeuvres. Grieve, H. 1944
Sprint from the bell. Booth, P. 1966
Spur of morning. Mulgan, A. 1934
Stamper Battery. Howe, A. 1964
Stand in the rain. Watson, J. 1965
State of siege, A. Frame, J. 1967
Stations. Temple, P. 1979
Statues. Billing, G. 1971
Stepping stones with a rebel. Mutch, K. 1973
Stinson's Bush. Macdonald, G. 1954
Stormy possession. Bianchin, H. 1979
Storrington papers, The. Eden, D. 1979
Story of a New Zealand river, The. Mander, J. 1920
Story of a New Zealand sheep farm. Cherrill, A. 1950
Story of Jody, The. Mutch, K. 1970
Story of Wild Will Enderby, The. Pyke, V. 1873
Strange attraction, The. Mander, J. 1922
Strange friendship, A. Evans, C. 1874
Strange horizon. Lusk, E. 1934
Stranger, The. Saunders, G. 1978
Stranger from Shanghai. Staples, M. 1968
Stranger stands, A. Owen, D. 1964
Stranger to the truth. Sanderson, N. 1969
Strangers. Ewing, B. 1978
Strangers and journeys. Shadbolt, M. 1972
Strangers for tea. Scott, M. 1975
Streak of gold, A. Clair, D. 1978
Strictly speaking. Scott, M. 1969

Strip Jack naked. Wilson, G. 1957
Stubble field, The. Winder, M. 1956
Such nice people. Scott, M. 1962
Sugar heaven. Devanny, J. 1936
Sullen bell, The. Davin, D. 1956
Summer at Awakopu. Donald, R. 1978
Summer in December. Summers, E. 1970
Sun at noon. Hill, J. 1956
Sun breaks through, The. Sanderson, N. 1975
Sun is God, The. Noonan, M. 1973
Sunlit seas. Preston, I. 1977
Sunset village. Sargeson, F. 1976
Surfeit of Lampreys. Marsh, N. 1940
Surgeon in New Zealand, A. Sava, G. 1964
Sweet white wine. Wilson, G. 1956
Swing brother swing. Marsh, N. 1949
Swords and crowns and rings. Park, R. 1977
Sydney Bridge upside down. Ballantyne, D. 1968
Symbol of vengeance. Mariner, D. 1975
Syndicate, The. Rhodes, D. 1960

Tail of the Dozing Cat, The. Messenger, E. 1965
Tainted money. Manning, A. 1963
Take any city. Joseph, G. 1970
Tale of a trooper, The. McKenzie, C. 1921
Talisman for a bride. Berg, R. 1976
Talk back man, The. Ballantyne, D. 1978
Tamarask in bloom. Preston, I. 1963
Taming of Nurse Conway, The. Sanderson, N. 1964
Tangahano. Keinzly, F. 1960
Tangi. Ihimaera, W. 1973
Tapu tree, The. Carman, D. 1954
Taranaki. Stoney, H. 1861
Target for malice. Cooper, E. 1964
Tarry knight! Allen, C. 1927
Tar white. Tullett, J. 1962
Taunt from the past, A. Swift, R. 1970
Tempered wind, The. Fenwick, M. 1964
Tenth home, The. Bennett, F. 1966
Te Rou. White, J. 1874
Terese. Andrews, P. 1967
That Gibbie galoot. Gibson, H. 1924
That summer. Sargeson, F. 1943
That summer's dolphin. Shadbolt, M. 1969
That summer's earthquake. Bennett, M. 1963
That was the hour. Thwaites, F. 1956
There and back. Crump, B. 1963
These dark glasses. Texidor, G. 1949
They called her Faith. Lusk, E. 1932
They will arise. Uren, M. 1945
This man's father had my father's farm. Hammond, T. 1966
This Mrs Kingi. Cleary, F. 1971
This spring of love. Mergendahl, C. 1948
Thousand pities, A. Taylor E. 1901
Three. Ashton-Warner, S. 1970
Three strings to a fortune. Worboys, A. 1962
Three women. Reyburn, W. 1960

Through all the years. Summers, E. 1974
Thunder Beach, Grayland, V. 1972
Ticket of destiny. Preston, I. 1969
Tidal creek. Finlayson, R. 1948
Tides of youth. Scanlan, N. 1933
Tied up in tinsel. Marsh, N. 1972
Tiger of Baraguna, The. Emery, J. 1924
Tikera. Wishniowski, S. 1877
Time and the place, The. Summers, E. 1964
Time of Achamoth, The. Joseph, M. 1977
Time of the dragon, The. Eden, D. 1975
Time to die, A. Pothan, K. 1967
Time to prey, A. Keinzley, F. 1969
Toll of the bush, The. Satchell, W. 1905
Tonks. Church, H. 1916
Tomorrow's sun. Carman, D. 1964
Top step, The. Scanlan, N. 1931
Torn tapestry. Gordon, M. 1929
To the garden alone. Burfield, E. 1970
Touch of clay, A. Shadbolt, M. 1974
Town of fear. Tullett, J. 1970
Tracks we tread, The. Lyttleton, E. 1907
Tragedy of a flirtation, The. Vogel, H. 1909
Transgressions of Aolele, The. Sadd, N. 1940
Travelling man. McClenaghan, J. 1976
Tree without shade. Jeffery, M. 1971
Trial and error. Joseph, G. 1979
Trip to New Zealand, A. Bosworth, I. 1930
Troop target. Fullarton, J. 1943
Troup of star-crossed killers, A. Journet, T. 1973
Tryphena's summer. Owen, W. 1974
Tune and the dancer, The. Macdonald, S. 1936
Turkey at twelve. Scott, M. 1968
Turn of the tide, The. Johnson, M. 1968
Tussock fever. Fernandez, N. 1973
Tussock land. Adams, A. 1904
Two faces of Nurse Roberts, The. Sanderson, N. 1963

Uncertain quest. Messenger, E. 1965
Unchanging love, The. Quentin, D. 1959
Under one standard. Bedford, H. 1916
Under palm and pine. Owen, J. 1919
Unwritten book, The. Scott, M. 1957
Utu. Bullock, M. 1894

Valiant love. Myers, M. 1941
Valley in the clouds. Addison, D. 1963
Valley of yesterday, The. Worboys, A. 1965
Venetian inheritance. Worboys, A. 1973
Via Panama. Jepson, M. 1934
Vicissitudes of bush life. Ferguson, D. 1891
Victim. Journet, T. 1974
Vines in splendour, The. Bianchin, H. 1978
Vintage murder. Marsh, N. 1937
Visit to Penmorten, The. Courage, J. 1961
Visit to Rata Creek. Worboys, A. 1964
Voice from the cell. Mackenzie, A. 1961
Voyage of destiny. Preston, I. 1974

Voyagers, The. Shadbolt, M. 1967
Voyagers in aspic. Gillies, J. 1954

Wages of desire. Devanny, J. 1930
Waihoura. Kingston, W. 1869
Waitaruna. Bathgate, A. 1881
Waiting for Willa. Eden, D. 1970
Wanted a son. Adair, H. 1935
War to the knife. Browne, T. 1899
Watersiders, The. Davis, M. 1964
Way of love, A. Courage, J. 1959
We love you Nurse Peters. Phipps, G. 1974
We never die in winter. Manning, A. 1958
Web of the spider, The. Watson, H. 1890
Wednesday's children. Hyde, R. 1937
What does it matter? Scott, M. 1966
Wheat in the ear. Baker, L. 1898
When in Rome. Marsh, N. 1970
Where kowhai blooms. Moore, M. 1968
Where lies the land? Sanders, J. 1976
Where no roads go. Summers, E. 1963
Where ratas twine. Preston, I. 1960
Where the apple reddens. Scott, M. 1934
When the rainbow is pale. Joseph, G. 1962
When the wind blows. Sargeson, F. 1945
Whispering echo, The. McGregor, M. 1969
Whistle for the crows. Eden, D. 1962
White elephant, The. Scott, M. 1959
White for danger. Stevens, D. 1979
White man's shoes. Ruhen, O. 1960
White mantle. Owen, M. 1967
White orchid. Mason, H. 1953
White pine. Tullett, J. 1965
Whose candle is the sun. Joyce, T. 1963
Wife in exchange. Donald, R. 1979
Wildcat. Mutch, K. 1968
Willing heart, The. Bianchin, H. 1975
Wind and the rain, The. Hodge, M. 1936
Wind may blow. Hill, J. 1953
Winds of heaven. Scanlan, N. 1934
Winterwood. Eden, D. 1967
Witch's thorn, The. Park, R. 1951
With gently smiling jaws. Maddock, S. 1963
Witnesses, The. Holden, A. 1971
Women of the family, The. Phipps, G. 1956
Wooden rails. Smyth, W. 1930
Word for word. Muir, M. 1960
World is an orange and the sun, The. Watson, J. 1978
Wowser, The. Thornton, G. 1916
Wreath for Rivera, A. Marsh, N. 1949
Wreath for the Springboks, A. Calder, J. 1977
Wrong side of the door, The. Kennedy, M. 1963

Yanks are coming, The. Lee, J. 1943
Yellow fever. Wilson, T. 1979
Yellow flowers in the antipodean room. Frame, J. 1968
Yellow Jack's island. St. Bruno, A. 1963
Yellow kowhai. Burfield, E. 1957

Yes, darling. Scott, M. 1967
You know the way it is. Jones, A. 1956
You won't need a coat. Messenger, E. 1964
Young have secrets, The. Courage, J. 1954
Young pretender, The. Allen, C. 1939
Young summer, The. Scanlan, N. 1952
Young wife, The. Phipps, G. 1962
Youngest one, The. Carman, D. 1965
Yours to oblige. Scott, M. 1954

Zealandia's guerdon. Walker, W. 1902

Author Index

The dates in bold type refer to the year of publication of a novel. Titles and other information may be checked by cross-reference to the bibliography. Dates of birth and death are given where known.

ABERDEIN, John Keith. **1977**
ACHESON, Frank Oswald Victor, 1887-1948. **1930**
ADAIR, Hazel, pseudonym of Hazel Iris Addis (Wilson). **1935**
ADAMS, Arthur Henry, 1872-1936. **1904, 1912**
ADAMS, R. N. **1897**
ADDISON, Doris Maureen (Bentley), b.1926. **1963, 1964, 1965**(2), **1967**(2)
ADSETT, Delphin Rose, wrote as Dell Adsett, b.1920. **1963, 1974**
ALLEN, Charles Richard, 1885-1962. **1926, 1927, 1936, 1937, 1939**
ALLEY, Rewi, b.1897. **1973**
ANDREWS, Isobel Smith (Young). **1969, 1971**
ANDREWS, Philip. **1967**
ANTHONY, Frank Sheldon, 1891-1925. **1936, 1938, 1951, 1952, 1955, 1963, 1975, 1977**
ARCHIBALD, Menie. **1963**
ARETA, Mavis, see Winder, Mavis.
ARMFELT, Nicholas. **1971**
ASHTON-WARNER, Sylvia Constance, Mrs Henderson. **1958, 1960, 1964, 1966, 1970**
AUDLEY, Ernest Henry, b.1895. **1963, 1965**
AYLMER, Mrs Isabella. **1862**

BACON, Ronald Leonard, b.1924. **1963, 1964**
BAGLEY, Desmond. **1975**
BAINES, William Mortimer, 'W.M.B.', d.1912. **1874**
BAKER, Heretaunga Pananehu Pat. **1975**
BAKER, Louisa Alica (Dawson), pseudonym 'Alien', 1858-1926. **1894, 1898**
BALDWIN, Beatrice Lilian, b.1920. **1965**
BALLANTYNE, David Watt, b.1924. **1948, 1963, 1966, 1968, 1978**
BARKER, Lady Mary Anne, 1831-1911. **1872**
BATES, Peter. **1966, 1968, 1970, 1973**
BATHGATE, Alexander, 1845-1930. **1881**
BAUME, Frederic Ehrenfried, wrote as Eric Baume, 1900-1967. **1933, 1934, 1947, 1949, 1953**
BEDFORD, H. Louisa. **1916**
BELL, George William, 1832-1907. **1904**
BELL, John. **1899**

BENJAMIN, Philip. **1964**
BENNETT, Francis Oswald, b.1898. **1966, 1971**
BENNETT, Margot, b.1912. **1963, 1968**
BERG, Rilla, pseudonym of Thelma France. **1974, 1976, 1977**(2), **1978, 1979**
BERROW, Norman. **1934**
BEVAN, Gloria. **1965, 1969**(2), **1970, 1971**(3), **1973, 1974**(2), **1975, 1976, 1977**(2), **1978**
BIANCHIN, Helen S. **1975, 1976, 1977, 1978, 1979**(2)
BIGGAR, Joan. **1977**
BILLING, Graham John, b.1936. **1965, 1968, 1971, 1973**
BLISS, Alice, b.1925. **1969**
BOLITHO (Henry), Hector, 1898-1974. **1927, 1929, 1930, 1946**
BOOTH, Patrick John, b.1929. **1961, 1964, 1965, 1966**
BOSWELL, John. **1958**
BOSWORTH, Isabel. **1930**
BRATHWAITE, Errol Freeman, b.1924. **1959, 1961, 1964**(2), **1965, 1967**
BRENT, Marama. **1961, 1970**
BRITTON, Anna. **1977**
BRODIE, Gordon. **1968**
BRODIE, John, see Guthrie, John.
BROWN, J. Edward, b.1929. **1963**
BROWN, John Macmillan, pseudonym Geoffrey Sweven, 1846-1935. **1901, 1903**
BROWNE, Charles Robert Barton, 1860-1932. **1929**
BROWNE, Thomas Alexander, pseudonym Rolf Boldrewood, 1826-1915. **1899**
BRUCE, John Merlin Copplestone, b.1938. **1977**
BULLOCK, Margaret (Carson), pseudonym Tua-O-Rangi, 1845-1926. **1894**
BURDON, Randall Mathews, 1896-1965. **1943**
BURFIELD, Eva, pseudonym of Mrs Frances Eva Ebbett, b.1925. **1957, 1958, 1964, 1969, 1970**
BURGESS, Michael, b.1925. **1964**
BURKE, David, b.1927. **1967**
BUTLER, Samuel, 1835-1902. **1872, 1901**

CALDER, Jason, pseudonym? **1976, 1977, 1978**
CAMERON, Ian. **1958**
CAMPBELL, Lady. **1864**
CAMPBELL, Margot, b.1911. **1954**
CAMPION, Edith, b.1923. **1979**
CARELL, Victor, b.1916. **1960**
CARMAN, Dulcie, i.e. Edith Marie Dulce
  Drummond (Carman), b.1883. **1924, 1948, 1950,
  1954, 1962(2), 1963, 1964(2), 1965, 1966, 1967**
CASEY, R., pseudonym of Kenneth Robert Christian,
  b.1929. **1963**
CATHIE, Diarmid Cameron, pseudonym, b.1910.
  1953
CHAMIER, George T., 1842-1915. **1891, 1895**
CHAPMAN, R. H. **1888**
CHEESMAN, Clara E., b.1852. **1886**
CHERRILL, Amy Lilian. **1950**
CHURCH, Hubert Newman Wigmore, 1852-1943.
  1916
CHURCHWARD, William Brown, 1845-1920. **1892**
CLAIR, Daphne, pseudonym of Daphne de Jong.
  1977, 1978(3), 1979(3)
CLAPPERTON, Annie Ada (Reeves). **1936**
CLARKE, Mrs Neva Yvonne. **1964**
CLEARY, Frances. **1971, 1975**
CODY, Joseph Frederick, 1895-1967. **1955**
COLLEY, I. B. **1974**
CONSTABLE, Lawrence. **1973**
COOK, Harvey Harold. **1925, 1927**
COOP, Harold Valentine, wrote as Harold Valentine.
  1964
COOPER, Mrs Evelyn Barbara. **1964**
COTTLE, Thomas, 1845-1923. **1891**
COUMBE, Eric Edwin. **1965**
COURAGE, James Francis, 1903-1963. **1933, 1950,
  1952, 1954, 1956, 1959, 1961**
COWLEY, Cassia Joy (Summers), b.1936? **1967,
  1970, 1972, 1975, 1978**
CRAWFORD, James Temple. **1978**
CRISP, Frank. **1956**
CROSS, Ian Robert, b.1925. **1957, 1960, 1961**
CRUMP, Barry John, b.1935. **1960, 1961, 1962,
  1963, 1964, 1965, 1967, 1970, 1971, 1972**
CRUMP, Walter William. **1964**

DAVIES, George Pearce. **1975**
DAVIN, Daniel Marcus, b.1913. **1945, 1947, 1949,
  1956, 1959, 1970, 1972**
DAVIS, George Harold, b.1892? **1974**
DAVIS, Michael Henry Lester, b.1931? **1962, 1964**
DAVIS, Thomas Robert Alexander, b.1918. **1960**
DE MAUNY, Erik Cecil Leon, b.1918. **1949**
DENMAN, Peter. **1973**
DEVANNY, Jean, i.e. Jane? (Crooks), 1894-1962.
  1926(2), 1928, 1929, 1930(2), 1932, 1936, 1942
DEVERELL, Evangeline. **1909**
DINGWELL, Joyce. **1963, 1975**

DONALD, Robyn, pseudonym of Mrs Robyn
  Kingston. **1977, 1978(2), 1979(2)**
DORIEN, Ray. **1956**
DORMAN, Thomas Edwin, b.1914. **1969, 1975**
DRESCHFELT, Mrs, wrote as Prudence Cadey.
  1933
DRYLAND, Gordon Boyce, b.1926. **1965, 1973(2)**
DUCKWORTH, Marilyn Rose (Adcock) b.1935.
  1959, 1960, 1963, 1969
DYKES, Mervyn Ian, b.1942. **1978**
DYSON, John. **1974**

EBBETT, Eve or Eva, see Burfield, Eva.
EDEN, Dorothy, b.1912. **1940, 1948, 1952, 1953,
  1954, 1960, 1962, 1963, 1964, 1965, 1966, 1967,
  1970, 1972, 1974, 1975, 1977, 1979**
ELDRED-GRIGG, Stevan Treleaven. **1977**
ELLIOTT, Sir James Sands, 1880-1959. **1939**
ELLIS, Ellen E. **1882**
ELLIS, Michael, pseudonym of Stephen Peter
  Llewellyn, 1913-60. **1957, 1960**
EMERY, J. Inman. **1924**
ESCOTT, Margaret, 1908-77. **1936**
EVANS, Mrs Charlotte. **1874(2)**
EWEN, J. M. **1966**
EWING, Barbara Jean, b.1939. **1978**
EYRE, Annette, see WORBOYS, Anne (Eyre).

FAGAN, Elizabeth. **1965**
FAIRBURN, Edwin, pseudonym 'Mohoao',
  1827-1911. **1867**
FARJEON, Benjamin Leopold, 1838-1903. **1865,
  1866**
FENTON, Elizabeth. **1957**
FENWICK, Margaret. **1964**
FERGUSON, Sir Bernard Edward, b.1911. **1972**
FERGUSON, Carlyle. **1913**
FERGUSON, Dugald, 1833-1920. **1891, 1912**
FERGUSON, Henry. **1932**
FERNANDEZ, Natalie. **1973**
FINLAYSON, Roderick David, b.1904. **1948, 1953**
FISHER, Bert. **1976, 1977, 1978**
FLAXMAN, Anna. **1941**
FORDE, H. A. **1896**
FOSTON, Herman. **1921**
FOWLER, Percy Leo, b.1902. **1959**
FRAME, Janet Paterson, b.1924. **1957, 1961, 1962,
  1963, 1965, 1967, 1968, 1970, 1972, 1979**
FRANCE, Helena Ruth, 1918-1968. **1958, 1961**
FRANCIS, Charles, see Peters, Charles.
FRANCIS, Dick. **1976**
FRASER, A. A. **1888**
FULLARTON, John Haydn, 1908-78. **1943**
FUSSELL, James Coldham, 1874-1945. **1918**

GANT, Phyllis. **1973, 1976**

GARFORD, James. **1961**
GARLAND, Stuart. **1954**
GEDGE, Pauline, b.1945. **1977**
GEE, Maurice Gough, b.1931. **1962, 1965, 1972, 1976, 1978**
GEE, Wallace. **1964**
GEDDES, Adrienne Marie (Kelliher). **1964**
GIBBONS, Margaret (Macgill). **1918**
GIBSON, Colin. **1970, 1971**
GIBSON, Harry Thomas, 1876-1957. **1924**
GILBERT, Gavin Robert, b.1917. **1952**
GILBERT, Manu, pseudonym? **1967**
GILLIES, John Russell, b.1920. **1954**
GLENDAY, Alice. **1973**
GLOVER, Denis, b.1912. **1978**
GORDON, Mona Clifton. **1929**
GOUDGE, Elizabeth, b.1900. **1944**
GRACE, Alfred Augustus, 1867-1942. **1908, 1914**
GRACE, Patricia Frances, b.1937. **1978**
GRAHAM, Timothy, M. A., b.1939. **1969**
GRAY, Alison Margaret, wrote as Ailsa Gray. **1979**
GRAYLAND, Valerie Merle (Spanner), also wrote as Lee Belverdere. **1962, 1963, 1964, 1965, 1971, 1972(2), 1973**
GREENWOOD, Helene (Fordor), 1878-1932. **1931**
GRIEVE, Mrs Hamilton, b.1902. **1944, 1947, 1950**
GRIFFIN, Andrew Dow, b.1884. **1961**
GROSSMANN, Edith Howitt (Searle), 1863-1931. **1910**
GROVER, Raymond Frank, b.1931. **1967**
GURR, Thomas Stuart. **1958**
GUTHRIE, John, pseudonym of John Brodie, 1905-55. **1935, 1936, 1949, 1950(2), 1952(2)**

HALES, Alfred Greenwood, 1870-1936. **1917**
HALL, J., 'J.H.L.' **1892**
HAMMOND, Theodore Peter. **1966**
HANSEN, Ole Conrad, 1871-1947. **1935**
HARRISON, Craig, b.1942. **1976**
HARVEY, Norman Bruce, b.1931. **1963, 1967**
HAYTER, Adrian Goodenough, b.1914. **1977**
HAYWARD, Rudall Charles Victor. **1939**
HEATH, M. **1978**
HELLIER, F. **1915**
HELLIWELL, Arthur. **1974**
HENAGHAN, Rosalie. **1970**
HENDERSON, Michael Ronald, b.1942. **1975**
HENSHAW, William Keith. **1964**
HENTY, George Alfred, 1832-1902. **1890**
HEWETT, Joan Evelyne, b.1912. **1937**
HILL, Jean O'Hagan (Morton), 1904?-68. **1953, 1956, 1963**
HILLIARD, Noel Harvey, b.1929. **1960, 1965, 1969, 1970, 1978**
HOARE, Hugh Alan. **1973**
HODDER, William Reginald. **1903, 1933**

HODGE, Merton, i.e. Horace Emerton Hodge, 1903?-58. **1936**
HOGG, James Wilson. **1934**
HOLCROFT, Montague Harry, b.1902. **1928, 1929, 1931, 1936**
HOLDEN, Anne Jacqueline (Dare), b.1928. **1965, 1967, 1968, 1971, 1973**
HOLDER, William Graeme, 1890?-1944. **1931**
HOLMES, Robert Barry. **1979**
HOLT, Sheila Betty (Archibald), wrote as Betty Holt. **1965**
HOOD, Archibald. **1890**
HOOKER, John. **1971**
HOOPER, Peter. **1979**
HORSELY, Reginald Ernest, 1863-1926. **1907**
HOUGHTON, Philip. **1966**
HOUSE, L. C. (Lesley), pseudonym of Elsie Macleod-Smith. **1964**
HOWE, A. **1964**
HUGHES, Ivy Rose (Hay), wrote as Catherine Hay, b.1910. **1962, 1963, 1964, 1966, 1968, 1970**
HUME, Fergus, b.1849. **1896**
HUNTER, Edward, 1885-1959. **1920**
HUNTER, Harriet. **1966**
HURNE, Ralph. **1963**
HUTCHINSON, Ivy. **1971**
HYDE, Robin, pseudonym of Iris Guiver Wilkinson, 1906-39. **1936(2), 1937, 1938(2)**

IHIMAERA, Witi Tame, b.1944. **1973, 1974**
INGLEWOOD, Kathleen, Kate Evelyn (Isitt), b.1876. **1905**

JACKSON, Francis. **1951, 1952, 1955, 1963**
JACKSON, Laurence. **1969**
JAY, Simon, pseudonym of Dr. Colin James Alexander, b.1921. **1964, 1968**
JEFFERY, Margaret, i.e. Gretchen Constance Emilie (Weyergang). **1955, 1964, 1971, 1973**
JEPSON, Margaret. **1934**
JOHNSON, Marguerite Maud, wrote as Rewa Glenn. **1964, 1968**
JONES, Arthur Edwin, b.1911. **1956**
JOSEPH, George Israel, b.1912. **1957, 1962, 1963, 1970, 1979**
JOSEPH, Michael Kennedy, b.1914. **1958, 1962, 1967, 1976, 1977**
JOURNET, Terence Harry. **1967, 1968, 1973, 1974**
JOYCE, Thomas Heath. **1963**

K., J. H., pseudonym. **1872**
KAYE, Mrs Eliza Bannerman. **1900**
KEINZLY, Mrs Frances, also spelt Keinzley, b.1922. **1960, 1969, 1970**
KELLY, Maurice. **1972**
KENNEDY, Marion. **1963**
KENNY, Alice Annie, 1875?-1960. **1934**

KENYON, Frank Wilson, b.1912. **1955, 1961**
KERR, Walter. **1926**
KIDMAN, Fiona. b.1940. **1979**
KING, David, see Quentin, D. **1950**
KINGSTON, William Henry Giles, 1840-80. **1869,**
   1869?
KOCH, Claude F. **1965**
KOEBEL, William Henry, 1872-1923. **1908**

LAMBE, Zoe Violetta (Lane). **1967**
LANCASTER, G. B., see Lyttleton, Edith.
LANGFORD, Gary Raymond, b.1947. **1976**
LANGTON, William. **1889**
LAWLOR, Patrick Anthony, 1894-1979. **1938**
LAWSON, Will, 1876-1957. **1945, 1946, 1951**
LAY, Graeme John, b.1944. **1978**
LEE, John Alexander, b.1891. **1934, 1936, 1937,**
   1943, 1944, 1964, 1970, 1975, 1976
LINDSAY, Kathleen, b.1903. **1959**
LLOYD, Victor Stanton, b.1898. **1930**
LOCKLEY, Ronald Mathias, b.1903. **1974**
LORD, Albert Fawcett. **1957**
LUSK, Elizabeth (Rees), pseudonym Elizabeth
   Milton. **1932, 1934**
LUSON, Pamela. **1971**
LYNN, David, pseudonym of D. McLennan. **1943**
LYTTLETON, Edith Joan, pseudonym G. B.
   Lancaster, 1873-1945. **1907, 1908, 1933, 1938**

McADAM, Constance (Clyde), wrote as Constance
   Clyde, b.1872. **1905**
McCARTHY, Darry, b.1928. **1956**
MacCARTIE, Justin Charles. **1891**
McCLENAGHAN, John Nathaniel, b.1929? **1966,**
   1969, 1976
McCLYMONT, Margot Kate, 1887-1959. **1956, 1958**
MACDONALD, Georgina Bruce (Blaikie), 1906-59.
   1949, 1954
MACDONALD, Sheila (Mackenzie), later Mrs S. S.
   Moore. **1936**
McGREGOR, Miriam Florence. **1968, 1969**(2), **1970,**
   1971(2)
MACKAY, Mrs Margaret Elizabeth. **1963**
McKENNY, Kenneth, b.1929. **1965, 1970, 1972**
MACKENZIE, Andrew Carr, b.1911. **1948, 1961**
McKENZIE, Sir Clutha Nantes, 1895-1966. **1921**
MACKERSEY, Ian, b.1925. **1955, 1974**
McLEOD, Mrs Catherine Styles. **1967, 1970**
McLEOD, Rosemary, b.1950? **1976**
McNEISH, James Henry Peter, b.1931. **1970, 1976**
MACKRELL, Brian Heslop. **1975**
MACTIER, Susie, i.e. Susan (Seaman). **1908, 1911**
MADDOCK, Shirley Francis Whitley, b.1932. **1963**
MAKGILL, Sir George, 1868-1926. **1903**
MANDER, (Mary) Jane, 1877-1949. **1920, 1921,**
   1922, 1925, 1926, 1928
MANN, Catherine. **1955, 1956**
MANNING, Arthur, b.1919. **1958, 1960, 1963, 1973**

MANSFIELD, Katherine, Kathleen Murry
   (Beauchamp), 1888-1923. **1979**
MANTELL, Lorraine, wrote as Laurie Mantell. **1978**
MARINER, David. **1975**
MARRYATT, Emilia. **1874**
MARSH, Dame (Edith) Ngaio, b.1899. **1934, 1935**(2),
   1936, 1937, 1938(2), **1939, 1940**(2), **1942, 1943,**
   1944, 1947, 1949, 1951, 1953, 1955, 1956, 1958,
   1959, 1962, 1964, 1966, 1968, 1970, 1972, 1974,
   1977, 1978
MASON, Colin. **1973**
MASON, Francis van Wyck, b.1901. **1969**
MASON, Henrietta Rex. **1953, 1960, 1963, 1966**
MASON, Hugh. **1976**
MAUGHAN, C. William, b.1940. **1974**
MERGENDAHL, Charles Henry, b.1919. **1948**
MESSENGER, Elizabeth, i.e. Betty Margery (Esson),
   1908?-1965. **1958, 1959, 1960, 1962, 1963, 1964**(2),
   1965(2)
MICHAEL, Shona, b.1934. **1970**
MIDDLETON, Ian, b.1928. **1979**
MIDDLETON, Osman Edward Gordon, b.1925.
   1979
MINCHER, Philip R. **1977**
MITCALFE, Barry, b.1930. **1975**
MITCHELL, June Ellis, b.1918. **1978**
MONCRIEFF, Perrine (Millais). **1976**
MOORE, Mary. **1968, 1969, 1971, 1973, 1974**(2)
MORRIESON, James Ronald Hugh, 1922-72. **1963,**
   1964, 1974, 1976
MOUNTAIN, Julian, b.1908. **1946, 1948**
MUIR, Macgregor Robin, b.1918. **1960**
MULCOCK, Anne. **1971**
MULGAN, Alan Edward, 1881-1962. **1934**
MULGAN, John Alan Edward, 1911-45. **1939**
MUSGROVE, H. **1917**
MUTCH, Karin. **1968, 1969, 1970, 1971**(2), **1973**
MYERS, Martha Washington. **1941**

NEATE, Frank Anthony, b.1929. **1966**
NETHERCOTE, Ron. **1970**
NEWTON, Peter, b.1906. **1972**
NISBET, Hume, b.1849. **1896**
NOONAN, Michael. **1958, 1963, 1969, 1973**

O'HAGAN, Joan. **1976**
OLLIVIER, Mrs Sally T. b.1910. **1965**
O'NEILL, David Patrick, b.1946. **1975**
OSMOND, Sophie. **1922**
O'SULLIVAN, Katherine (Morgan), 1881-1962. **1948**
O'SULLIVAN, Vincent Gerard, b.1937. **1976**
OWEN, Charles. **1905**
OWEN, Doreen May, b.1928. **1964, 1965**
OWEN, Jean Allan (Pinder), 1841-1922. **1919**
OWEN, Maurice. **1967**
OWEN, William. **1974**

PAOLOTTI, John, *see* Wilson, Guthrie. **1963**

PARK, Rosina Ruth Lucia, Mrs D'Arcy Niland, wrote as Ruth Park. b.1919. **1948, 1949, 1951, 1953, 1955, 1957, 1961, 1977**

PARVIN, Brian. **1979**

PEACOCKE, Isabel Maud, Mrs Cluett, b.1881. **1918, 1920, 1923, 1946, 1950**

PEARSON, William Harrison, b.1922. **1963**

PEEL, Colin Dudley. **1973(3), 1976, 1977, 1978**

PENBERTHY, Brent. **1972**

PETERS, Charles, wrote as Charles Francis, b.1921. **1963, 1964(2)**

PFLAUM, Melanie (Lowenthal), b.1909. **1974, 1975, 1977**

PHIPPS, Grace Mary (Palk), b.1901. **1955, 1956, 1962, 1963, 1969, 1971, 1972, 1973, 1974, 1976, 1978**

PLATTS, Herbert Walton. **1911**

POTHAN, Kap. **1967**

POWELL, John D. **1979**

PRESTON, Florence Margaret, b.1905. **1956, 1957, 1958, 1959**

PRESTON, Ivy Alice (Kinross), b.1914. **1960, 1962, 1963(2), 1964, 1965, 1968, 1969(2), 1970, 1973, 1974(2), 1976(2), 1977, 1978, 1979**

PRIESTLEY, Clive Brian, b.1926. **1977, 1978**

PRIOR, Ann, b.1949. **1969**

PYKE, Vincent, wrote as F. E. Renwick, 1827-94. **1868, 1873, 1874, 1884**

QUENTIN, Dorothy, Mrs Madeleine Batten, wrote also as Linda Beverly, b.1911. **1941, 1949, 1950(2), 1953, 1955, 1959, 1960, 1963, 1969**

RAY, James. **1932**

RAWLINSON, Gloria, b.1918. **1839**

REED, Alexander Wyclif, see Hayward, R. **1939**

REED, George McCullagh, 1832-89. **1889, 1896**

REES, Rosemary Frances, 1876-1963. **1924(2), 1925, 1927, 1931(2), 1936, 1938, 1940, 1947, 1956, 1958, 1962**

REES, Arthur John, b.1872. **1913**

REEVES, Amber, pseudonym of Mrs. White. **1911**

REYBURN, Wallace. **1956, 1957, 1960, 1962**

RHODES, Denys, b.1919. **1952, 1960**

RICHMOND, Mary. **1940**

RITCHIE, Kevin W. b.1930. **1972**

ROBERTSON, J. R. **1978**

ROBERTSON, Mrs Rita Clarice, b.1913. **1964, 1965**

ROCK, Gilbert. **1889**

ROGERS, Ray Mount. **1960**

ROOKE, Daphne Marie, b.1914. **1969**

RUHEN, Olaf, b.1911. **1958, 1960, 1965, 1969**

S.S. **1965**

SADD, Norman, pseudonym. **1940**

SAFRONI-MIDDLETON, Arnold, 1873?-1950. **1923**

ST. BRUNO, Albert Francis, wrote as Frank Bruno, 1910-67. **1959, 1960, 1962, 1963, 1966**

SALTER, Elizabeth. **1957**

SANDERS, James Edward, b.1911. **1971, 1972, 1973(2), 1975(2), 1976, 1978**

SANDERSON, Nora (Brocas), b.1905. **1962, 1963(2), 1964(3), 1965, 1968(2), 1969, 1970, 1971, 1975**

SANDFORD, Kenneth Leslie. **1955**

SANDYS, Elspeth, Mrs Bruce Purchase. **1978**

SARGENT, Winston. **1945**

SARGESON, Frank, b.1903. **1943, 1945, 1949, 1952, 1965, 1967, 1969, 1972(2), 1976, 1979**

SATCHELL, William, 1860-1942. **1902, 1905, 1907, 1914**

SAUNDERS, G. K. **1978**

SAVA, George, pseudonym of George Alexis Milkomanovich Milkomane, b.1903. **1964**

SCANLAN, Nelle Margaret, 1882-1968. **1931(2), 1932, 1933, 1934, 1935, 1936, 1937, 1938, 1939, 1944, 1946, 1948, 1950, 1952**

SCOTT, Gavin, b.1950. **1977**

SCOTT, Mary Edith (Clarke), 1888-1979. **1936, 1954, 1960, 1962, 1963(2), 1964(2), 1965(2), 1966, 1968, 1969, 1970, 1972, 1974, 1975, 1977, 1978**

SCOTT, Nicholas D., b.1925. **1966**

SCOTT, Robert H. **1895**

SHADBOLT, Maurice Francis Richard, b.1932. **1965, 1967, 1969, 1971, 1972, 1974, 1975**

SHORTLAND, Edward George, 1855-1929. **1885**

SIMONS, Wendy. **1979**

SIMPSON, Roger, b.1944, see Dykes, M. **1978**

SLATTER, Gordon Cyril, b.1922. **1959, 1968**

SLIGO, John, b.1944. **1978**

SMITH, Harry Gilmore. **1936**

SMITH, Michael L. **1962**

SMYTH, Walter. **1928, 1929, 1930**

SNELLER, Jean. **1969**

SOPER, Eileen Louise (Service). **1971**

SPENCER, Earle. **1978**

STAPLES, Marjory Charlotte (Jefcoate), wrote as Rosaline Redwood, b.1912. **1941, 1966, 1967, 1968**

STEAD, Christian Karlson, b.1932. **1971**

STELIN, Ebba. **1896**

STEPHENSON, Ralph. **1963, 1966**

STEVENS, David. **1979**

STONEY, Henry Butler, 1816-94. **1861**

STRINGFELLOW, Mrs Olga, b.1923. **1959**

STUART, Marten, see Scott, M. **1934, 1935**

SUMMERS, Essie, pseudonym of Ethel Snelson Flett. **1957, 1959, 1963(2), 1964(3), 1968, 1969(2), 1970(2), 1971(2), 1973, 1974(2), 1975, 1976, 1977(2), 1978(2), 1979(2)**

SUTHERLAND, James Hector, b.1925. **1978**

SUTHERLAND, Margaret, b.1941. **1974, 1976**

SUTTON, Phyllis. **1958**

SWIFT, Rachelle, pseudonym of Jean Lumsden. **1969, 1970, 1971, 1972, 1973**

TARRANT, Noeline. **1965**

TATE, Robert Desmond. **1933**

TAYLOR, Brian. **1975**
TAYLOR, Ellen. **1901**
TAYLOR, William, b.1940? **1970**(2), **1971**, **1972**(2), **1974**
TEMPLE, Philip. **1975**, **1979**
TEXIDOR, Greville, Mrs Droescher, 1902-64. **1949**
THIAN, Valerie Joan. **1970**
THOMAS, William Hearn, b.1870. **1963**
THOMPSON, Nola Dilyse (Payne), b.1927. **1966**
THORNTON, Guy. **1916**
THWAITES, Frederick Joseph. **1956**
TINDALE, Norman Barnett, b.1900. **1959**
TOWNSHEND, Don J. **1975**
TRAVIS, Neal. **1979**
TREGEAR, Edward, 1846-1931. **1895**
TULLETT, James Stuart. **1962**, **1964**, **1965**, **1966**, **1970**

UREN, Martyn. **1945**

VERNE, Jules Gabriel, 1828-1905. **1868**, **1888**(2)
VOGEL, Harry Benjamin, 1868-1947. **1898**, **1909**
VOGEL, Sir Julius, 1835-99. **1889**

WALKER, William Sylvester, 1846-1926. **1902**
WALLIS, Redmond Frenkton, 1933? **1962**
WALSH, Mrs Hazel. **1947**
WARDON, Reve. **1892**
WATSON, Henry Brereton Marriott, 1863-1921. **1890**
WATSON, Jean Catherine. **1965**, **1975**, **1978**
WEDDE, Ian Curtis, b.1946. **1976**
WENDT, Albert, b.1939. **1973**, **1977**, **1979**
WEST, Joyce. **1936**, and with Mary Scott **1960**, **1962**, **1963**, **1964**, **1965**
WESTBURY, F. Atha. **1896**
WESTON, Jessie, 1868-1944. **1890**
WHITE, John, 1826-91. **1874**, **1940**
WHITE, Nelia (Gardner), b.1894. **1942**
WHITWORTH, Jess. **1950**
WHITWORTH, Robert P. **1887**
WHYTE, Anna D. **1935**, **1936**
WILKINSON, Iris, see Hyde, Robin.
WILLIAMS, Harley, i.e. John Hargreaves Harley, b.1901. **1941**
WILLIAMS, Robert J. **1979**
WILLS, Cecil Melville, b.1891. **1955**
WILSON, Lady Anne Glenny (Adams), 1848-1930. **1893**
WILSON, George Hamish, 1833?-1905. **1874**
WILSON, Guthrie Edward Melville, b.1914. **1950**, **1952**, **1954**, **1956**, **1957**, **1959**, **1960**, **1963**
WILSON, Helen Mary (Ostler), 1874-1957. **1944**, **1955**
WILSON, Phillip John, b.1922. **1963**, **1964**, **1965**, **1973**, **1976**
WILSON, Trevor Edward. **1971**, **1972**, **1973**, **1977**, **1979**

WINDER, Mavis Areta (Wright), b.1907. **1955**, **1956**, **1962**, **1963**, **1964**, **1965**, **1967**, **1968**, **1969**, **1973**
WINGATE, March. **1955**
WISNIOWSKI, Sygurd, 1841-92. **1877**
WORBOYS, Anne (Eyre), wrote as Annette Eyre. **1962**(2), **1964**, **1965**, **1966**, **1970**, **1971**, **1973**, **1975**
WORDSWORTH, Jane. **1972**, **1975**
WRIGHT, Stanley Sherman. **1936**
WYLIE, Cicely. **1966**
YAGER, Marie J. **1956**

References

BURNS, James Alexander Scott. *A century of New Zealand novels, a bibliography of the period 1861-1960.* Auckland, Whitcombe & Tombs, 1961. iv, 26p.

BURNS, J. New Zealand writing 1964. (*In* Books abroad, vol. 39, no. 2, spring 1965, pages 152-155.)

BURNS, J. *New Zealand writing 1965; a bibliography.* Auckland, Rothmans, 1966. 6p, folder.

BURNS, J. New Zealand literary scene. (*In* Books abroad, vol. 41, no. 3, summer 1967, pages 288-291.)
(Books abroad is an international literary quarterly published by the University of Oklahoma. Since 1977 it has had the title 'World literature today'.

CURNOW, Wystan, editor. *Essays on New Zealand literature.* Auckland, Heinemann Educational Books, 1973. viii, 192p.

DAVIN, Daniel Marcus. The New Zealand novel... (*In* the Journal of the Royal Society of Arts, vol. 110, no. 5072, July 1962, pages 586-598.)

GRIES, Joan Corbett. *An outline of prose fiction in New Zealand.* Thesis for Ph.D. in English. Auckland, 1951. 2 vols.

HANKIN, Cherry, editor. *Critical essays on the New Zealand novel.* Auckland, Heinemann Educational Books, 1976. xvi, 170p.

HOCKEN, Thomas Morland. *Bibliography of New Zealand literature.* Wellington, Government Printer, 1909. xii, 619p.

HOLCROFT, Montague Harry. *Islands of innocence; the childhood theme in New Zealand fiction.* Wellington, Reed, 1964. 63p.

HORNCY, Janet and Catherine Hutchinson, compilers. *New Zealand fiction October 1957-1968; an annotated list of novels and collected short stories.* Wellington, N.Z. Library School, 1968. 70 leaves.

Index to New Zealand periodicals and Current national bibliography. Wellington, National Library Service, 1940- . Since 1967 issued as New Zealand national bibliography.

Islands, a New Zealand quarterly of arts and letters. Edited and published by Robin Dudding, Auckland. 1972- .

Journal of Commonwealth literature. Heinemann Educational Books and The University of Leeds. September 1965- .

Landfall, a New Zealand quarterly published by The Caxton Press, Christchurch. 1947- .

McCORMICK Eric Hall. *New Zealand literature; a survey.* London, Oxford University Press, 1959. 173p.

MILLEN, Elizabeth M. M. *New Zealand fiction 1947-1957; an annotated list of novels and short stories.* Wellington, New Zealand Library School, 1957. 11 leaves.

NEW ZEALAND LIBRARY ASSOCIATION. Fiction list; monthly supplement... Wellington, National Library of New Zealand for the New Zealand Library Assn.

NEW ZEALAND NATIONAL BIBLIOGRAPHY to the year 1960. Editor and principal compiler A. G. Bagnall. Wellington, Government Printer, 1969, i.e. 1970. Vol. 1 (published 1980), vol. 2, 1890-1960, A-H. Vol. 3, 1890-1960, I-O. Vol. 4, 1890-1960, P-Z.

PEARSON, William Harrison. *Fretful sleepers and other essays.* Auckland, Heinemann Educational Books, 1974. viii, 168p.

REID, John Cowie. *Creative writing in New Zealand; a brief critical history.* Auckland, printed for the author by Whitcombe and Tombs. 1946. 93p.

RHODES, Harold Winston. *New Zealand fiction since 1945; a critical survey of recent novels and short stories.* Dunedin, John McIndoe, 1968, 64p.

RHODES, H. Winston. *New Zealand novels; a thematic approach.* Wellington, New Zealand University Press, Price Milburn. 1969. 71p. (Studies in New Zealand literature.)

SMITH, Elizabeth Maisie. *A history of New Zealand fiction, from 1862 to the present time with some account of its relation to the national life and character.* Wellington, Reed, 1939. 101p.

STEVENS, Joan. *The New Zealand novel 1860-1965.* Second revised edition to 1965. Wellington, Reed, 1966. 159p. First edition 1961.

VOLKERLING, Michael. *Images of society in New Zealand writing; an examination of the social concerns of New Zealand writers 1960-1970.* Auckland, 1975. 265 leaves. Thesis for Ph.D. in English, University of Auckland.